TRANSLATION WORKSHOP
翻译工作坊

周亚莉　朱瑾瑞　邓　洁　编著

U0914005

蘭州大學出版社
LANZHOU UNIVERSITY PRESS

图书在版编目（C I P）数据

翻译工作坊 / 周亚莉，朱瑾瑞，邓洁编著. -- 兰州：兰州大学出版社，2021.7
ISBN 978-7-311-05982-8

Ⅰ. ①翻… Ⅱ. ①周… ②朱… ③邓… Ⅲ. ①英语－翻译－教材 Ⅳ. ①H315.9

中国版本图书馆CIP数据核字(2021)第068426号

责任编辑　陈红升
封面设计　汪如祥

书　　名　翻译工作坊
作　　者　周亚莉　朱瑾瑞　邓　洁　编著
出版发行　兰州大学出版社　（地址：兰州市天水南路222号　730000）
电　　话　0931-8912613（总编办公室）　0931-8617156（营销中心）
　　　　　0931-8914298（读者服务部）
网　　址　http://press.lzu.edu.cn
电子信箱　press@lzu.edu.cn
印　　刷　西安日报社印务中心
开　　本　710 mm×1020 mm　1/16
印　　张　12.5
字　　数　220千
版　　次　2021年7月第1版
印　　次　2021年7月第1次印刷
书　　号　ISBN 978-7-311-05982-8
定　　价　42.00元

前　言

“工作坊”（workshop）这一概念最早起源于教育与心理学研究领域，指一个小的群体就某个创造性项目或课题进行深入调查研究或讨论。“翻译工作坊”就是一群从事翻译活动的人聚集在一起，就具体的翻译任务进行讨论，并最终选择大家均认可的译文。作为一门交互性极高的课程，“翻译工作坊”已被多所高校纳入翻译专业课程体系，是面向翻译专业本科学生的专业限选课之一。以学生为主体的翻译工作坊教学模式顺应教育部“专创融合”要求，旨在进一步提升学生的创新型高阶思维。该教学模式需配备实践型与专业化较强的配套教材，但目前翻译工作坊教材都偏向理论与文学领域，无法有效地模拟翻译实践的真实情境。本教材在此背景下应运而生。

基于“以人为本”的现代教学思想，本教材以培养学生高层次、应用型、专业性翻译思维与翻译能力为核心，在结构安排、内容设置、选材范围、翻译实践等方面均遵循“时代性、实践性、职业性”原则。本教材的绪论部分共分为三节，分别介绍了“翻译工作坊”“项目式教学法在翻译教学中的实施”及“翻译项目质量评估”，以厘清本书的重点概念。此外，该部分还根据项目管理的九大知识领域呈现了翻译项目管理及相关策略，并提供《翻译质量评估标准表》。基于翻译项目管理的概念，本教材建构了“医学翻译”“文化翻译”“外事翻译”“经济翻译”“教育翻译”“科技翻译”“新闻翻译”“体育翻译”“法律翻译”“人物简介翻译”“演讲辞翻译”“旅游翻译”“学术翻译”“工程翻译”和“历史文献翻译”15个单元主题。每个单元的第一节为“背景知识与文本特点”，介绍相关定义分类及文本特点，并指出对应的翻译原则与技巧；第二节为“专业术语与常用表达”，网罗各类专业术语与常用表达，以表格形式呈现，方便读者查阅；第三节和第四节分别为“英译汉翻译实务”与“汉译英翻译实务”，分别选取学生的初稿修改稿和最终稿，以真实体现翻译项目管理过程；第五节为“翻译项目质量评估”，从词法句法和语篇三方面对所选译文进行评析；后为“课外拓展”，根据每一单元的主题设计了相关口译情境，延伸课外实践。此外，编者在每单元后提供的参考文献旨在拓宽学习者视野，提供更多阅读资料。

本教材特点如下：

1.时代性——教材充分挖掘各专业领域的双语素材，题材广泛素材新颖难度适中译例典型，适合小组合作讨论完成；

2.实践性——教材以实践为主，理论为辅，配合翻译工作坊的教学流程，模拟真实翻译情境，实现了翻译教学的实践路径；

3.职业性——教材顺应当今社会对翻译人才能力的需求，引导学生参与翻译项目的整体流程，积累翻译经验，树立译者身份意识，确立未来的职业规划，从而提升学习者的翻译职业能力素养。

本书适用于作为翻译专业本科生的教材或教辅，也适合翻译公司的从业人员、政府外事部门的翻译人员和广大翻译爱好者以作翻译辅助材料。

本教材由西北师范大学外国语学院教授周亚莉、甘肃省兰州第一中学英语教师朱瑾瑞和西安外国语大学翻译学博士邓洁共同编著。周亚莉负责全书各章主题确定、章节结构安排、资料选摘与统筹和内容审校。朱瑾瑞负责绪论的撰写和第一章至第七章各节的内容编写，邓洁负责第八章至第十五章各节的内容编写。本教材各章的第三、四节的学生译文初稿、修改稿、终稿均选自编者在2020年春季学期“笔译工作坊”课程中的模拟翻译项目，特此感谢西北师范大学外国语学院2017级翻译系1班和2班同学的配合。

本教材为2020年甘肃省高等学校英语教学改革项目“基于高阶思维型教学模式的《笔译工作坊》教学改革研究”（W202015）成果之一。

本教材绪论中有关翻译项目管理的编写重点取材于黄忠廉的《翻译项目管理》。特此说明，并向黄教授致以诚挚的谢意！

由于编者水平有限，时间仓促，笔下疏漏在所难免，敬希专家同行和读者不吝赐教，使之日趋完善。

编　者

2021年1月

目　录

绪　论

一、翻译工作坊

传统的翻译课堂多将学生视为分离的个体，单独进行翻译任务。教师修改学生译文成为翻译课堂上仅有的交流。虽然这种教学方式具有针对性，但无法有效培养学生的团队协作能力。单人翻译已经无法满足现代社会发展快节奏的需求，多人合作翻译逐渐形成一种主流的翻译模式，存在于社会翻译实践之中。无论中国还是西方，都曾出现过大规模的多人合作翻译活动，如中国的佛经翻译和西方的圣经翻译，相较于单人翻译，多人翻译模式具有效率高的优势，在翻译过程中，译者能及时交流，分享心得，集思广益。因此，多人模式的主要组织形式能为翻译课堂提供具体可行的策略和方法。

“工作坊”最早源于德国魏玛共和国时期的包豪斯学院，学院创建者格拉皮乌斯（Walter Gropius）倡导“技艺与艺术并重”的教育理念，教学过程中应该注重实践，让学生成为课堂中心，教师负责辅助指导。以此为基础形成的教学模式被称为“工作坊教学”。“翻译工作坊”（Translation Workshop）正是引入了这一模式，将一群从事翻译活动的人聚集在一起，分工协作，完成翻译任务。该群体通过合理的任务分配、广泛的讨论协商，从而议定出所有成员均认可的译文。将翻译工作坊的模式引入翻译课堂，能够培养学生职业翻译素养，增强协作翻译能力，提高课堂翻译效率。

二、项目式教学法在翻译教学中的实施

16世纪末，意大利的建筑教育中开始实行项目教学法。18世纪，欧洲建筑和工程学院引进该教学法，毕业生须利用所学到的理论知识和技能，解决建筑工程中的实际问题。1918年，美国教育学家克伯屈（Kilpatrick）界定了广义上的“项目教学法”（Project Method），指出这是一项有目的、处于实际环境的学习活动。21世纪，基于建构主义理论的项目式教学法（Project-based Learning，简称PBL）得到推广，并逐渐运用至翻译教学中。针对翻译实践的项目式教学法是学生在所构建的真实环境中，通过项目合作完成任务。基于项目式教学法的“翻译工作坊”课程教学，可训练学生在未来工作环境中解决翻译实践问题的能力。

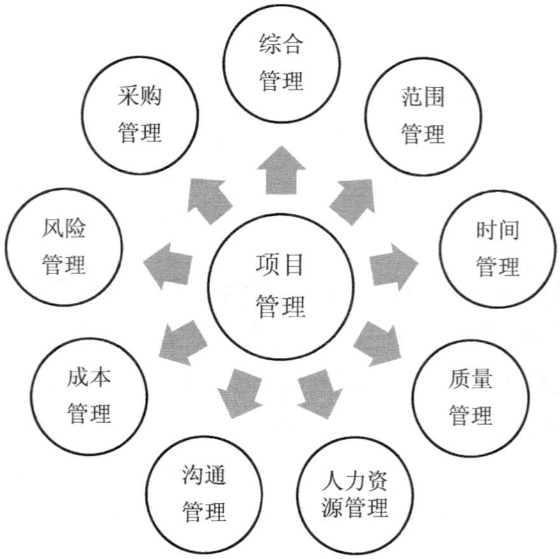

图1 项目管理知识体系（源自：《翻译项目管理》）

基于图1所示的有关项目管理的九大知识领域，翻译项目管理及策略具体如下：

序号	名称	内容	策略	备注
1	综合管理	(1)项目计划书：项目章程、工作范围说明、工作分解结构、时间计划、人员计划、风险识别、约束和假设、存在的问题等。	建立项目文档。这有助于组织项目的顺利进行。笔译项目应建立以下关键文档：项目合同、项目质量要求参数、项目组织结构、工作分解结构、项目进度表、项目沟通计划、项目风险评估、项目进度报告、项目验收报告、项目客户满意度调查报告和项目总结报告。	
		(2)执行流程：计划和执行流程、计划执行反馈流程、问题搜集和解决流程、决策流程、需求变更管理流程、设计变更管理流程。		
		(3)变更控制：对变更流程执行的控制。		
		(4)经验教训：项目各个阶段完成后的总结。		
2	范围管理	(1)项目章程：项目目标、需求描述、任务项目经理。	项目请求方和翻译服务方应共同认可并承诺项目目标，包括项目工作范围的确定、质量需求和具体实施规划的可行性等，并尽量与在翻译参数分析基础上制定的项目规范保持一致。	
		(2)工作范围说明：尽可能详细列出翻译的具体要求和工作内容、验收标准，以便取得预期的效果。		
		(3)范围变更控制：对工作范围（需求和设计）变更流程执行的控制。		

续表

序号	名称	内容	策略	备注
3	时间管理	(1)项目进度计划:根据目标进行行动排序、行动历时估算,然后再根据可用的译、审、排等资源情况,合理制定项目进度计划。 (2)计划管理方法:执行计划、执行反馈、流程控制、时间进度、分析进度趋势。	必要时分解工作任务,可根据项目的规模和工作内容将项目分解为不同的子项目,或主要工作项目和次要工作项目,子项目还可分为不同的工作单元,并对每一个单元进行进度管理。	
4	成本管理	(1)人员工作量记录。 (2)采购费用记录,包括设备、场地、服务的采购费用。在笔译项目中,通常指的是外包的翻译、审校、排版、后期编辑等相关费用。	应根据不同的项目制定最优化的流程,以达到用最小成本保质保量地完成项目。需要充分了解可用资源的质量、工作速度、工作能力等,才能实现团队的最佳组合。比如,一个驾照或者身份证的小件翻译,就无需译、审、排三道工序,也无需走复杂的项目流程,而应该建立绿色通道,以最快速度完成工作,否则管理成本会远高于翻译成本。	
5	质量管理	(1)规范:质量规范、文档排版规范等。 (2)质量计划:制定质量标准及达到质量标准的方法。 (3)后续支持模式。	为项目实施过程中的每一个关键人员,如译员、审校和排版制定重点质量检查表,明确在每一个要点需要"检查"的"质量"是什么,并保证质量检查反馈及时。在项目进程中,客户的参与度对提升项目的总体质量至关重要,所以精明的客户,应懂得如何在项目中参与质量管理,甚至调集整合一些可利用的资源来帮助翻译的团队解决一些稿件中的难点问题,督促和协助项目团队更好地完成项目任务。	
6	人力资源管理	(1)编制组织结构图; (2)编制角色和责任; (3)建立项目规章制度; (4)团队建设相关策略。	对于很多翻译公司来说,笔译项目的团队成员都有外部兼职译员、审校、排版等相关资源的参与。团队成员通过互联网建立远程虚拟项目组协同合作,为了提升凝聚力,团队成员应该定期或者不定期地组织团队建设活动。比如,项目启动前召开启动会(Kick-off Meeting),可以用网络电话会议的形式召开。如果有条件,可以组织兼职成员和内部专职人员的交流会和集中培训,团队成员见面后进行远程合作时,明显会感觉沟通更顺畅,更容易接受和理解对方。	

续表

序号	名称	内容	策略	备注
7	沟通管理	(1)沟通计划:明确各类沟通方法、对象、频度等。 (2)工作成果记录。 (3)简报。 (4)电子邮件、微信、腾讯QQ等快速通信方式。	翻译服务过程中,项目经理有时要面对和处理客户方的投诉。当客户提出异议时,项目经理的关键行动是正确判断问题症结所在,这需要项目经理以平和的心态耐心倾听各方陈述,然后找出问题出现的真正原因,及时解决。切不可情绪化行事,或者偏听偏信,最终导致双方误会摩擦增大,演变成纠纷。	
8	风险管理	(1)风险识别; (2)风险应对计划;	预测和分析项目风险,监督每个项目环节的质量控制流程及其实施过程,发现质量问题,立即采取补救措施,在过程中控制项目质量风险。项目进展过程中若出现与项目计划不符的工作范围、进度和费用的变化,需及时调整项目管理流程,并及时向项目干系人发布变更方案。	
9	供应商管理	(1)采购合同:选择合适的合同类型。 (2)供应商管理计划(供应商评估、合同管理):制定供应商评估标准表。	供应商和采购方是合作关系,基于双方的彼此尊重和认可,合作方可持续。因此,供应商的选择、价格确定、工作流程的安排、协议的签订等细节都要慎重处理。对于大型翻译公司,绝对不能只有1-2个供应商,所谓“不能把所有的鸡蛋都放在一个篮子里”。必须要不断开发新的更为优秀的供应商,才能保持自己的话语权。其次,良好的服务意识之于翻译项目管理有着举足轻重的地位。有时客户方提出不尽合理的要求或者提出诉讼等,项目经理要本着解决问题的出发点,积极寻求解决方案。因此,项目经理与质控专家一起与客户方质量负责人召开会议,就客户提出的问题进行面对面的沟通。	

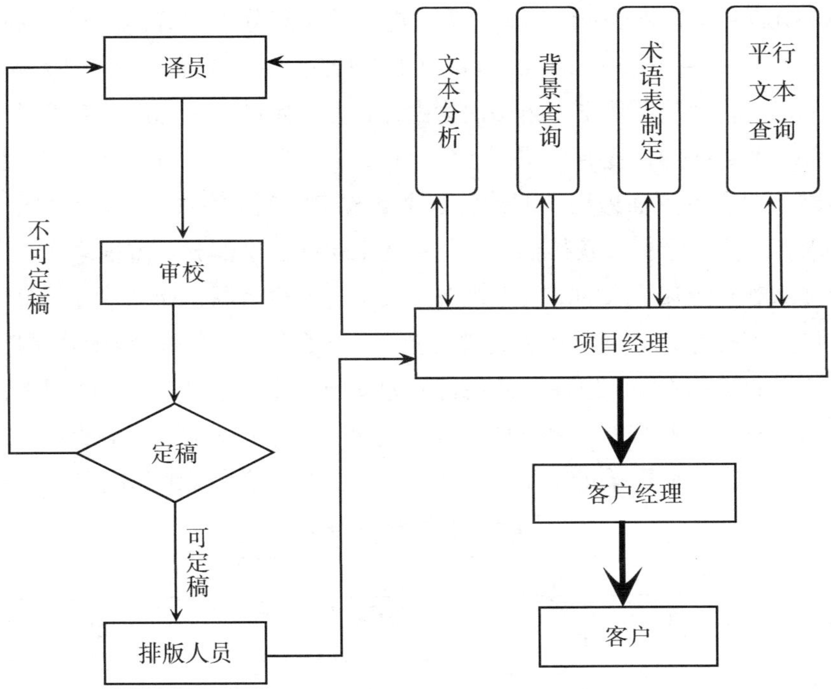

图2　翻译项目翻译流程图

翻译项目分为译前、译中、译后三个阶段。在译前阶段，项目经理分别安排人员从词法、句法、语篇等角度进行文本特点分析；查询有关文本的背景知识并制定术语表；查阅平行文本，掌握同类型文本的翻译策略及方法，从而保证译前准备工作的有序进行，实现翻译项目前期的质量控制。项目经理将所有翻译文本相关资料打包发给译员，安排译员进行翻译；在译中阶段，译员完成翻译任务，相互审校后再发给审校人员；在译后阶段，审校人员结束审校工作后，可根据审校结果决定是否定稿，如果错误较多，须将译文返至译员。译员再次修改译文，审校人员进行二次审校，以保障译文质量，最终将定稿发给排版人员。排版人员根据客户要求进行排版之后，交付项目经理，再经由客户经理将最终定稿提交至客户，从而完成整个翻译项目流程。

三、翻译项目质量评估

2002年起,中国翻译行业协会下属的翻译服务委员会开始组织和编制翻译服务行业的国家标准，并由国家标准化管理委员会颁布实施《翻译服务规范第1部分：笔译》(Specification for Translation Service-Part1: Translation-GB/T19363.1-2003)、《翻译服务译文质量要求》(Target Text Quality Requirements for Translation

Services-GB/T19682-2005)和《翻译服务规范第2部分：口译》(Specification for Translation Service--Part 2:Interpretation-GB/T 19363.2-2006)。《翻译服务规范第1部分：笔译》作为我国历史上第一次为翻译行业制定的国家标准，对翻译服务单位的条件、业务接洽、业务标识、业务流程、质量要求、资料保存、用户反馈和质量跟踪、保密等方面做出了明确的定义和规定。2005年3月，《翻译服务译文质量要求》作为国家标准获得批准，基本要求包括三个部分：重视原文、术语统一、行文通顺。特殊要求的范围涉及数字表达、专用名词、计量单位、符号、缩写词、译文编排等，并给出相关处理规范。《翻译服务译文质量要求》制定了译文质量评定的基本原则：以译文使用目的为基础，综合考虑其他关联因素，如原文文体和质量、专业难度、翻译时限等。此外，《翻译服务译文质量要求》还对译文质量的差错类别和译文综合差错率计算方法做了较为详细的规定。

翻译质量评估标准

错误类别	内容	质量扣分
语义理解错误	严重漏译和错译	5
	一般错译和漏译	4
	核心语义错误	4
	一般语义理解错误	3
	语法错误	3
术语错误	术语翻译不符合行业规范	3
	术语前后不符	1
文体风格错误	文体风格不符合特定文体	5
	译文前后措辞不符	2
其他错误	人名、地名等专有名词出现错误	1
	图表内容错误	1
	数字表达错误	1
	中英标点符号误用	1
	时间、计量单位错误	1
	其他排版格式错误	1

注：本表依据中华人民共和国国家标准《翻译服务译文质量要求（GB/T 19682-2005）》编制。

说明：1.出现严重漏译或误译现象，即译文逻辑不通，严重影响阅读效果，译文须返至译员重新修改润色。

2.同一语法错误重复出现，只记一次错误。

3.同一术语错误重复出现，只计一次错误；译文最多计三处术语错误。

4.其他错误项，每项计一次错误。

第一章　医学翻译

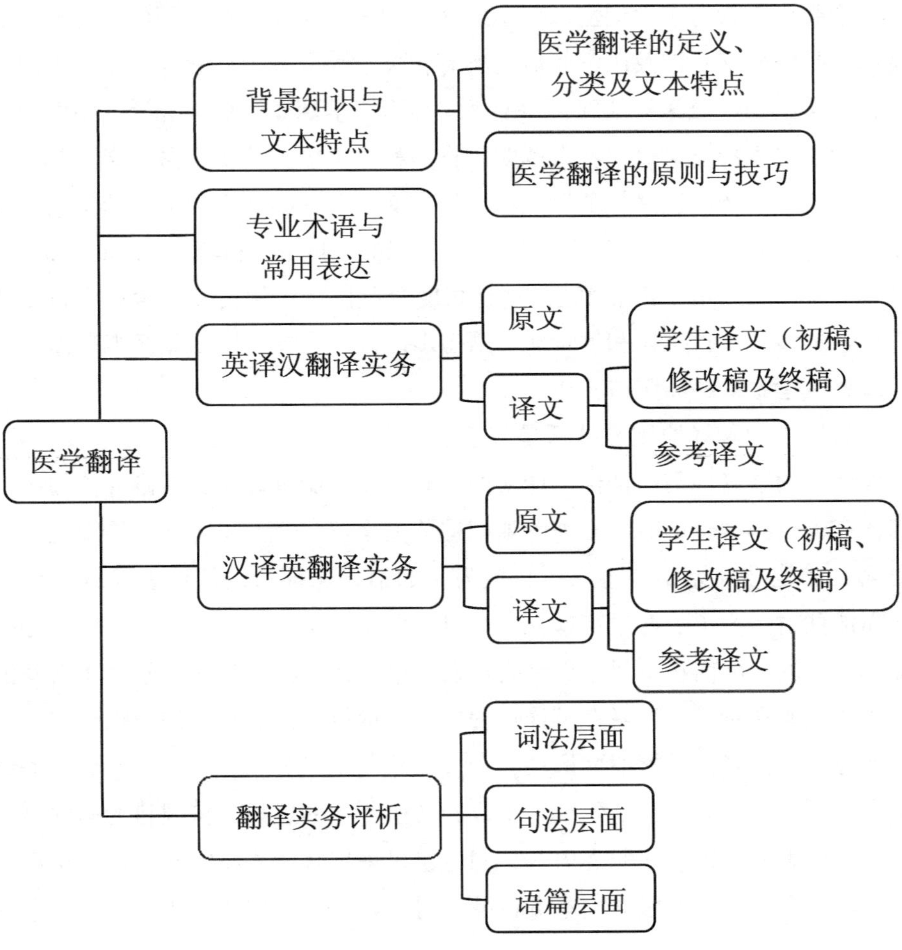
医学翻译
背景知识与文本特点
医学翻译的定义、分类及文本特点
医学翻译的原则与技巧
专业术语与常用表达
英译汉翻译实务
原文
译文
学生译文（初稿、修改稿及终稿）
参考译文
汉译英翻译实务
原文
译文
学生译文（初稿、修改稿及终稿）
参考译文
翻译实务评析
词法层面
句法层面
语篇层面

第一节 背景知识与文本特点

一、医学翻译定义、分类及文本特点

医学翻译特指对医学词汇、句子或文本的语际翻译。医学翻译的各分类名目下又涵盖具体分支，涉及医学领域的所有相关学科及分析试验等。根据不同医学领域，医学翻译可分为：基础医学翻译、临床医学翻译、药学翻译、中医药翻译等。医学类文本特征显著，特点鲜明。作为科技英语的分支，医学文本具有科技英语的客观性、严谨性和规范性。在词汇方面，医学类文本词汇来源复杂、词缀丰富，大部分词汇来源于拉丁语及希腊语，如：blenn（黏液）、blennogenic（黏液的），此类词汇词意相对稳定，具有高度专业性。医学类文本含有大量专业术语，表达上多使用长难句和复合句，语态多以被动为主，以凸显客观严谨。

二、医学翻译的原则与技巧

医学文本的翻译原则与技巧是基于医学文本特征及翻译目的而定的。首先，应确保译文的准确性与简洁性。译文的准确性是检验翻译工作者翻译能力的基础准则，在进行医学翻译时，必须清晰把握原文本信息、文本特征、语篇逻辑关系等要素，才能准确无误地将原语转换为目的语，保证目的语读者获取到无损信息。简洁性也是为了更好地传递原文信息，但切记不可为了简洁而简洁，必须在保证译文准确性的前提下尽量做到文本及术语表达简洁。基于医学文本自身的词汇、语法及句法特点，译者在翻译过程中可采取拆句法、重组法及综合法等翻译技巧及方法。译者需掌握原文语法，合理拆分句子成分，在通读全文后根据语法结构对句子进行划分，明晰句子主干成分及所传达的思想，按照目的语的表达习惯及特点准确简洁地表达原文内容，同时也可采用合译法将零碎的散句组成一个整句。简而言之，在对医学文本进行翻译时，译者可保留原文顺序，亦可采取变序的方式对原句进行重组。

第二节　专业术语与常用表达

ST	TT
1.新型冠状病毒	novel coronavirus
2.与感染者接触	contact with an infected person
3.生命重于泰山	saving lives is of paramount importance
4.医学排查	medical screening
5.CT影像	computed tomography imaging
6.防护服	protective suit
7.杜绝瞒报漏报	say NO to concealing or underreporting infections
8.防止疫情跨境传播	prevent the epidemic from spreading across boarders
9.居家隔离	home quarantine
10.可重复使用口罩	reusable mask
11.医疗用品和资源	medical supplies and resources
12.临床试验	clinical trails
13.抗病毒治疗	antiviral therapy
14.中西医结合	combined use of Traditional Chinese Medicine and Western Medicine
15.智慧医疗	Smart medical care
16.卫生系统	health system
17.流行病学史	historical epidemiology
18.交叉感染	cross infection
19.抗体检测	antibody detection
20.世卫组织驻华代表处	WHO China Representative Office
21.国际病毒分类委员会	International Committee on Taxonomy of Viruses (ICTV)
22.全球公共卫生安全	global public health security
23.定点医院	designated hospital
24.健康码	a health QR code
25.抗疫国际合作	international cooperation on fighting on COVID-19 outbreak

续表

ST	TT
26. 医护人员	medical personnel
27. 祝愿早日康复	May sb. get well soon./have an early recovery
28. 亟需	urgently needed
29. 新型冠状病毒肺炎	Novel Coronavirus Pneumonia
30. 核酸疫苗	nucleic acid vaccines
31. 确诊病例	confirmed case
32. 疑似病例	suspected case
33. 重症患者	patient in critical condition
34. 病死率	fatality rate
35. 轻型病人	people with mild disease
36. 科学战“疫”	science-based approach in fighting epidemic
37. 紧急救治	emergency treatment
38. 恢复正常医疗秩序	restoration of normal medical services
39. 医防结合	emphasis is needed on both prevention and treatment
40. 易感人群	susceptible/vulnerable population
41. 药品和疫苗研发	drug and vaccine development
42. 口罩正确佩戴、摘取及丢弃	the proper way to wear, remove and discard the mask
43. 含酒精的洗手液	alcohol-based hand sanitizer
44. 避免身体接触	avoid physical contact
45. 远程医疗	tele-medicine
46. 区域公共卫生应急联络机制	regional emergency liaison mechanisms
47. 中间宿主	intermediate host
48. 医学观察	medical observation
49. 无症状病人	asymptomatic patients
50. 医养结合	integration of medical treatment and elderly support

第三节　英译汉翻译实务

一、原文

Coronaviruses are a large family of viruses, some causing illness in people and others that circulate among animals, including camels, cats and bats. Rarely, animal coronaviruses can evolve and infect people and then spread between people such as has been seen with MERS and SARS.

Prevention Steps for Close Contacts:

If you have had close contact with someone who is confirmed to have, or being evaluated for, COVID−19 infection, you should:

Monitor your health starting from the day you first had close contact with the person and continue for 14 days after you last had close contact with the person.

· Watch for these signs and symptoms:

· Fever. Take your temperature twice a day.

· Coughing.

· Shortness of breath or difficulty breathing.

Other early symptoms to watch for are chills, body aches, sore throat, headache, diarrhea, nausea/vomiting, and runny nose.

If you develop fever or any of these symptoms, call your healthcare provider right away.

If you do not have any symptoms, you can continue with your daily activities, such as going to work, school, or other public areas.

二、学生译文初稿

冠状病毒是一大类病毒。其中有些病毒可能引起人类疾病，一些可能会在骆驼，猫和蝙蝠等多种动物之间传播动物冠状病毒，比如严重急性呼吸综合征冠状病毒以及中东呼吸综合征，动物冠状病毒极少进化和感染人类，进而在人与人之间传播。

密切接触者的预防措施:

如果你曾与已被证实或正在判断是否感染新型新冠肺炎，你应该做出以下措施，从你第一次与这个密切接触了那天起，居家隔离14天。

密切关注以下症状:

1.发烧，每天量两次体温。

2.咳嗽。

3.呼吸短促或呼吸困难。

4.其他需要注意的早期症状有寒战，身体疼痛，咽痛，头痛，腹泻，恶心或呕吐流鼻涕等。

若出现发烧或其它以上症状，立即拨打电话给医院或医护人员。

若无任何症状可继续工作学习等进行日常活动，可正常出入公共场所。

——译员：王鹏燕

三、学生译文修改稿

冠状病毒是一种大类病毒。其中有些病毒会引起人类疾病，而有些会在动物之间传播，包括骆驼、猫和蝙蝠等，，动物冠状病毒极少进化和感染人类，进而在人与人之间传播，比如严重急性呼吸综合征和中东呼吸综合症

密切接触者的预防措施:

如果您与已确认与患有冠状病毒感染或正在接受冠状病毒感染评估的人亲密接触，则应，从首次与该人亲切接触了那天起，监控状况，居家隔离 14 天。

注意以下体征和症状:

1.发烧。每天量两次体温。

2.咳嗽。

3.呼吸短促或呼吸困难。

4.其他您需要注意的早期症状有寒颤，身体疼痛，咽痛，头痛，腹泻，恶心或呕吐、流鼻涕等。

若出现发烧或其它以上症状，立即拨打电话给医院或医护人员。

若无上述任何症状可继续工作学习等进行日常活动，可正常出入公共场所。

删除[A]: 可能

删除[A]: 可能

删除[乔]: ，

删除[A]: 骆驼，猫和蝙蝠等多种动物之间传播动物冠状病毒

删除[A]: 比如严重急性呼吸综合征冠状病毒以及中东呼吸综合征，

删除[A]: 。

删除[A]: 你

删除[A]: 曾与已被证实或正在判断是否感染新型新冠肺炎，你应该做出以下措施

删除[A]: 你第一次

删除[A]: 这个密

删除[A]: 密切关注以下症状

删除[A]: 战

审校员：何丽霞

审校时间:2020.3.7

四、学生译文终稿

冠状病毒是一种大类病毒。其中有些病毒会引起人类疾病，而有些会在动物之间传播，包括骆驼、猫和蝙蝠等，动物冠状病毒极少进化和感染人类，进而在人与人之间传播，比如严重急性呼吸综合征和中东呼吸综合征。

密切接触者的预防措施:

如果您与已确认与患有冠状病毒感染或正在接受冠状病毒感染评估的人亲密接触，则应，从首次与该人亲切接触了那天起，监控状况，居家隔离14天。

注意以下体征和症状:

1.发烧。每天量两次体温。

2.咳嗽。

3.呼吸短促或呼吸困难。

4.其他您需要注意的早期症状有寒颤，身体疼痛，咽痛，头痛，腹泻，恶心或呕吐，流鼻涕等。

若出现发烧或其它以上症状，立即拨打电话给医院或医护人员。

若无上述任何症状可继续工作学习等进行日常活动，可正常出入公共场所。

审校员：何丽霞

审校时间:2020.3.7

五、参考译文

冠状病毒是一大类病毒，其中一些会导致人类患病，而另一些会在动物（包括骆驼、猫和蝙蝠）之间传播。在罕见情况下，动物冠状病毒能进化并感染人类，然后在人群中传播，例如在中东呼吸综合征（MERS）和严重急性呼吸道症候群（SARS）中所见到的情况。

密切接触者的预防措施：

如果您与已确诊患有COVID-19感染或正在接受COVID-19感染评估的患者有密切接触，您应从您第一次与患者密切接触之日开始监测您的健康状况，并在您最后一次与患者密切接触后继续监测您的健康状况 14 天。

观察以下这些体征和症状：

•发烧。每天两次测量您的体温。

•咳嗽。

•呼吸短促或呼吸困难。

其他需要注意的早期症状包括畏寒、身体疼痛、咽喉痛、头痛、腹泻、恶心、呕吐和流鼻涕。

如果您出现发热或以上任何症状，请立即致电您的医务人员。

如果您无症状，可以继续进行日常活动，如上班、上学或前往其他公共场所。

第四节　汉译英翻译实务

一、原文

联合国正与各国政府以及各合作伙伴保持密切合作，采购亟需的医疗用品和资源，支持中国的战疫工作。

我们也在探讨如何更好地支持中国在疫后的恢复，实现长期的社会与经济发展。目前，中国的卫生和教育系统正承受着巨大压力，我们随时准备提供支持，帮助这些领域早日恢复正常。

我敦促大家遵循世界卫生组织的指导：

互相问候时，请避免身体接触；

与人相见时，请与他人保持一米的距离；

务必经常用肥皂和水或含酒精的免洗洗手液洗手；

咳嗽或打喷嚏时，务必用纸巾遮住口鼻；

最后，请务必学习好口罩正确佩戴、摘取及丢弃的方法。

我还想借此机会，感谢所有在前线提供医疗卫生和紧急服务的工作人员，感谢他们为应对疫情做出的不懈努力。

我祝愿受到疫情影响的朋友们早日康复。

二、学生译文初稿

The United Nations is working closely with governments and partners to purchase much-needed medical supplies and resources to support China.

We are also exploring how to better support China's post-epidemic recovery and achieve long-term social and economic development. At present, China's health and education system is under tremendous pressure, and we are ready to provide support to help these areas return to normal as soon as possible.

I urge everyone to follow the guidelines of the WHO:

Avoid physical contact when greet each other;

Keep a safe distance of one meter from others when meet each other;

Wash your hands with soap and water or alcohol-free hand sanitizer;

Cover your nose and mouth with a tissue when coughing or sneezing;

Learn how to wear, remove, and discard masks correctly.

I would also like to take the path to thank all the staff who provided medical and emergency services on the front line, and thank them for their tireless efforts to respond to the outbreak.

I wish all patients who affected by the outbreak recovery.

——译员：王鹏燕

三、学生译文修改稿

The United Nations has a close cooperation with all governments and partners to procure needed -needed medical supplies and resources to support China's epidemic of coronavirus.

删除[A]: is working closely

删除[A]: purchase much

We are also exploring how to better support China's post-epidemic recovery and achieve long-term social and economic development. At present, China's health and education systems are under tremendous pressure, and we are always ready to provide support, to help these areas return to normal as soon as possible.

删除[A]: system is

I urge everyone to follow the guidelines of the W.H.O.:

删除[A]: WHO.:

Avoid physical contact when greet each other;

Keep a safe distance of one meter from others when meet each other;

Make sure to Wash your hands with soap and water or alcohol-free hand sanitizer;

Cover your nose and mouth with a tissue when coughing or sneezing;

Please make sure to learn how to wear, remove, and discard masks correctly.

I would also like to take the path to thank all the staff who provided medical treatment and public health and emergency services on the front line, and thank them for their tireless efforts for the epidemic.

删除[A]: medical

删除[A]: tirelees

删除[A]: to respond to

删除[A]: outbreak

I wish all patients who affected by the epidemic early recovery.

删除[A]: outbreak

审校员：何丽霞

审校时间：2020.3.7

四、学生译文终稿

The United Nations has a close cooperation with all governments and partners to procure needed-needed medical supplies and resources to support China's epidemic of coronavirus.

We are also exploring how to better support China's post-epidemic recovery and achieve long-term social and economic development. At present, China's health and education system are under tremendous pressure, and we are always ready to provide support to help these areas return to normal as soon as possible.

I urge everyone to follow the guidelines of the W.H.O.:

Avoid physical contact when greet each other;

Keep a safe distance of one meter from others when meet each other;

Make sure to wash your hands with soap and water or alcohol-free hand sanitizer;

Cover your nose and mouth with a tissue when coughing or sneezing;

Please make sure to learn how to wear, remove, and discard masks correctly.

I would also like to take the path to thank all the staff who provided medical treatment and public health and emergency services on the front line, and thank them for their tireless efforts for the epidemic.

I wish all patients who affected by the outbreak recovery.

审校员：何丽霞

审校时间：2020.3.7

五、参考译文

At the United Nations, we are working together with the government and partner to procure much-needed medical supplies and resources.

And we are also discussing how best to support China with the longer-term socio-economic impacts. In particular, we stand by to support the recovery of the health and education systems, which are under tremendous strain.

I urge all of you to follow the guidance of the World Health Organization:

•To greet each other without physical contact;

•Maintain a distance of one meter between you and others;

•Wash your hands frequently with soap and water or use hand sanitizer;

•Cover your mouth and nose with a tissue when you cough or sneeze;

•And finally, when you wear a mask, learn how to put it on, take it off and dispose of it correctly.

I also want to take this opportunity to commend all the frontline health and emergency service workers who are working tirelessly to respond to the outbreak.

And I wish all of you who are unwell a speedy recovery.

第五节　翻译实务评析

一、词法分析

词法是文本的基本元素，不同语言背景下的词汇在特定语境中有着不同的涵义，因此译者必须根据特定文本语境做出恰当选择。例如："you"在汉语中包含有"你、你们、您"等多种含义，基于中国谦逊有礼的文化传统，英译汉译文采用了最为合理的"您"。英语中有单复数之分，而汉语没有。因此译者在翻译过程中要根据语境灵活转换其单复数形式。例如，在"我敦促大家遵循世界卫生组织的指导"一句中，世界卫生组织的防疫指导不止一条，因而采用复数形式"guidelines"。此外，在"我祝愿所有受到疫情影响的朋友们早日康复"一句中"朋友们"体现了汉语委婉含蓄的特征，实指所有感染疫情的患者，为符合英语直白通透的语言特征，译文采用了其真实代指的"all patients"。

二、句法分析

在医学英语文本中多见长难句，而汉语常用短句及简单句，因此译者应适当使用拆译的方法进行翻译，以符合汉语的表达习惯。例如：原文（英译汉）第一段中，首句"Coronaviruses are a large family of viruses, some causing illness in people and others that circulate among animals, including camels, cats and bats."为长句，译者对原句结构重新划分，将原长句拆分为两个短句进行翻译，符合中英文句法特点。原文（汉译英）第一段中，"联合国正与各国政府以及各合作伙伴保持密切合作，采购亟需的医疗用品和资源，支持中国的战疫工作"这一句含有"保持"、"采购"和"支持"三个连续动词。经过译者分析，这三个动词并非并列关系，原句"保持密切合作"为主要信息，而"采购……"为保持合作的方式，"支持中国的战疫工作"为最终目的。因此，翻译成英语时，要注意体现其中的逻辑关系，采用不定式以表目的。在原文（汉译英）中，描述世界卫生组织的指导意见时，使用了五个并列的祈使句，用于警醒读者，因而译者采取直译法，遵循原文的语体特征和行文风格。

三、语篇分析

医学文本的专业性决定了其语篇的特殊性。总体而言，医学文本逻辑严谨，结构紧密，语篇内部衔接系统完整，这就要求译者在翻译实践过程中注重原文的完整性与同一性。原文属于信息型文本，以向读者传递信息为主。译文应尽量复制原语文本的语言形式，侧重“精准翻译”，重视准确无误地向读者传达原文信息。此外，代词的使用也是语篇逻辑性的重要体现。例如：原文（英译汉）“If you develop fever or any of these symptoms, call your healthcare provider right away.”中“these”一词用来指代上文中所提及的各种患病症状，在译文中译者将其处理为“以上”，增强了上下文的衔接，用语严谨凝练。

【课外拓展】

外籍友人在中国某医院接受核酸检测，请你担任陪同口译，与团队进行模拟情境表演。

文献参考

[1]贡璇．功能对等理论指导下医学英语翻译的句法研究[J]．继续医学教育，2018(12):58-59.

[2]贾德江．医学英语汉译方法初探[J]．中国科技翻译,1998(03):4.

[3]贾德江．周笃宝.医学英语阅读与翻译教程[M]．长沙:中南大学出版社，2002.

[4]黄忠廉．翻译项目管理[M]．北京:国防工业出版社,2014.

[5]林巍,赵友斌．医学翻译:词语与句式的辨析[J]．中国翻译,2019(03):181-184.

[6]黎昌抱,汪若然．试析合信医学翻译对近代中国西医翻译的贡献[J]．上海翻译,2020(01):45-49.

[7]王恬,医学术语新词的产生、构成及翻译[J]．继续医学教育,2013(06):31-35.

[8]叶子南．从深层和表层结构角度看医学翻译[J]．中国翻译,1986(02):40-42.

[9]郑岚．医学英语:特点与翻译策略[D]．上海:上海外国语大学,2007.

[10]张顺．拆译法和并句法在专门用途文本翻译中的应用[D]．大连:大连海事大学,2013.

[11]张志鸿．医学英语汉译技巧[M]．北京:人民卫生出版社,1983.

第二章　文化翻译

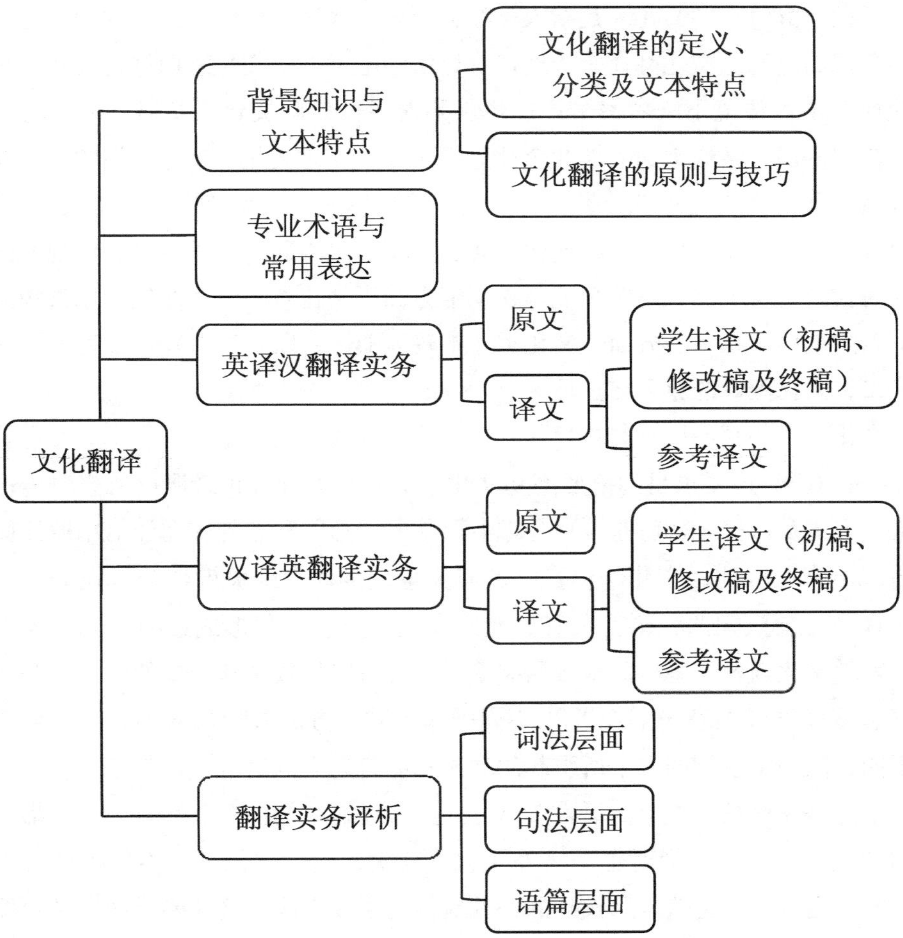
文化翻译
背景知识与文本特点
文化翻译的定义、分类及文本特点
文化翻译的原则与技巧
专业术语与常用表达
英译汉翻译实务
原文
译文
学生译文（初稿、修改稿及终稿）
参考译文
汉译英翻译实务
原文
译文
学生译文（初稿、修改稿及终稿）
参考译文
翻译实务评析
词法层面
句法层面
语篇层面

第一节　背景知识与文本特点

一、文化翻译定义、分类及文本特点

根据《辞海》，“文化”是指人类社会历史实践过程中创造出来的物质财富与精神财富的总和。文化翻译是指通过翻译活动把不同的文化意识进行转换，是在文化研究的大语境下来考察翻译，也就是对各民族间文化以及语言表达时“表层”与“深层”结构中的共性和个性进行研究，探讨文化与翻译之间的内在联系和客观规律。文化翻译各分类名目下又涵盖具体分支，涉及佛经、诗歌、俗语、小说等。文化类文本作为一种文化交融、互相学习沟通的手段，具有体现一国审美、时代特色、人文风情等功能。在词汇方面，文化类文本往往较为丰富华丽且用词斟酌准确。在句法方面，文化类文本较为随性，以表达内容含义为主。

二、文化翻译的原则与技巧

文化文本的翻译原则与技巧是基于文化翻译的目的而定。首先，忠实也就是文化“传真”。这要求目的语要遵从文化意义，从而准确再现源语所想要传达的含义、方式及风格。也就是说，是把源语中的“形”和“神”在译语中原汁原味地体现出来。因此，文化“传真”的研究也是翻译中的关键部分。在翻译的同时，译员也要熟知两种语言及其民族的发展历史、文化形成过程、风土人情传统、宗教文化以及一些特殊地域风貌等一系列可能导致文化差异的因素。著名美学家、翻译家朱光潜先生曾指出:不同国家不同地方的事物情境和人民的生活方式不同，同一个事物的文字所引起的联想和能打动人的兴趣点也就不同。不同的语言不论是在思维习惯上、语言表达方式上，还是在词汇意象和含义上，都有自己的特色，所以在翻译时也需格外注意。其次，文化“传真”不仅指忠实于原语，而且是兼顾文化差异后找到的一种最佳的翻译方法。这就要求译者必须探究词汇的渊源、社会背景意义以及此文化的深层含义，准确做到文化“传真”。不给“洋人”穿上“长袍马褂”，用最原汁原味的方式体现文化“传真”，准确把握好翻译中文化“传真”的度，而非过度生搬硬套。文化翻译最重要的策略为异化、归化。前者以源语文化为归宿，后者以目的语文化为导向。“异化”指的是译文应当尽量去匹配、遵从源语的文化和原作者的表达方式与风格。而“归化”则恰恰相反，其原则为译文应尽量匹配、遵从目的语的文化习惯，从读者的角度出发，为读者解决语言文化差异。总之，在考虑各国文化历史背景的前提下把

"信、达、雅"融为一体，使译文"神与形"并茂，这样才能确保文化"传真"的实现，真正做好文化翻译。

第二节　专业术语与常用表达

ST	TT
1. 十四行诗	sonnet
2. 散文诗	prose poem
3. 诗节	stanza
4. 颂诗	ode
5. 叙事诗	narrative poem
6. 打油诗	doggerel
7. 史诗	epic
8. 民谣	ballad
9. 谐音	euphony
10. 讽刺	satire
11. 明喻	simile
12. 拟人	personification
13. 暗喻、隐喻	metaphor
14. 押韵	rhyme
15. 重音	stress
16. 头韵	alliteration
17. 尾韵	end rhyme
18. 格律	Rules and forms of classical poem
19. 唐三彩	Tri-coloured Glazed Pottery of the Tang Dynasty
20. 刺绣	embroidery
21. 孝顺、孝心	filial piety
22. 祭祖、上供	offer sacrifices to ancestors
23. 网上祭扫	online tomb-sweeping
24. 门旁插柳	willow branches inserted on each gate
25. 中国精神、中国价值、中国力量	the Chinese Spirit, the Chinese Value and the Chinese Power
26. 打铁还需自身硬	It takes a good blacksmith to make good steel.
27. 最美逆行者	Heroes in harm's way
28. 没有硝烟的战争	a war without smoke

续表

ST	TT
29.英雄的城市	a heroic city
30.投我以木桃,报之以琼瑶	You throw a peach to me,I give you a white jade for friendship
31.疫情无国界,人间有真情	Virus knows no borders, but the worst of times reveals the best in people.
32.岂曰无衣,与子同裳	Together we stand, my armors thine.
33.山川异域,风月同天	miles apart but close at heart
34.同舟共济、守望相助	stick together through thick and thin
35.饮鸩止渴	seek temporary relief regardless of the consequences
36.民为国基,谷为民命	The people are the foundation of a country, food is the primary need of the people.
37.千里送鹅毛,礼轻情意重	It is the kindness that counts.
38.道不远人,人无异国	Great distance cannot separate us, we all live in a united world.
39.沧海横流,方显英雄本色	True heroes arise in times of hardship.
40.患难与共,共创未来	Supporting each other and acting together.
41.人心齐,泰山移	When people are determined, they can overcome anything.
42.挚友同心	Friendship is a single soul dwelling in two bodies.
43.修身、齐家、治国、平天下	Cultivate yourself, put your family in order, run the local government well, and bring peace to the entire country.
44.绿水青山就是金山银山	Lucid waters and lush mountains are invaluable assets.
45.青山一道,同担风雨(援助日本,源自王昌龄)	Like the mountain range that stretches before you and me, let's share the same trials and hardships together.
46.道不远人,人无异国(援助韩国,源自新罗旅唐学者崔致远)	Great distance cannot separate us; We all live in a united world.
47.亚当子孙皆兄弟,兄弟犹如手足亲。(援助伊朗,源自古波斯诗人萨迪)	The sons of Adam are limbs of one, having been created of one essence.
48.团结定能胜利。(援助法国,源自雨果)	United we shall overcome.
49.向疫情全面宣战	declare an all-out war on the epidemic
50.白衣执甲、逆行出征	Heedless of their own safety, medical workers headed for the frontline against the virus.

第三节　英译汉翻译实务

一、原文

Let me not to the marriage of true minds
Admit impediments. Love is not love
Which alters when it alteration finds,
Or bends with the remover to remove:
O no, it is an ever-fixed mark
That looks on tempests and is never shaken;
It is the star to every wandering bark,
Whose worth's unknown, although his height be taken.
Love's not Time's fool, though rosy lips and cheeks
Within his bending sickle's compass come:
Love alters not with his brief hours and weeks,
But bears it out even to the edge of doom.
If this be error and upon me proved,
I never writ, nor no man ever loved.

二、学生译文初稿

我相信，没有什么能阻碍
两颗真心的结合，
那种变化无常的情不是真情，
那种见异思迁的爱不是真爱。
噢，不！爱情是坚定不移的标志，
在狂风暴雨中从不动摇；
爱情是指引迷航船只的明星，
其高度可测但价值却无法估量。
真爱并不是傻傻的愚弄时间，
纵然朱唇红颜逃不过岁月的刀锋；
真爱并不因瞬时的改变而改变，
而是持之以恒直到天荒地老。

倘若我的话被证明是荒谬之言，
那就当我未曾写过诗，也无人真正爱过。

——译员：张云燕

三、学生译文修改稿

没有什么能阻碍
两颗真心的结合，
那种变化无常的情不是真情，
那种见异思迁的爱不是真爱。
噢，不！爱情是亘古长明的灯塔，
在狂风暴雨中从不动摇；
爱情是指引迷舟的明星，
其高度虽可测但价值却难估量。

真爱并不受时光的愚弄，
纵然朱唇红颜逃不过岁月的侵蚀；
真爱虽短暂，却至死不渝，持之以恒直到天荒地老。

倘若我所说的皆是谬论，
那就当我未曾写此诗，世上也无人真正爱过。

审校员：乔婷
审校时间：2020.3.15

删除[乔]：我相信，
删除[乔]：
删除[A]：坚定不移的标志
删除[A]：航船只
删除[乔]：无法
删除[乔]：是傻傻的愚弄时间
删除[乔]：刀锋
删除[乔]：并不因瞬时的改变而改变
删除[乔]：
而是
删除[乔]：的话被证明是荒谬之言
删除[乔]：过

四、学生译文终稿

没有什么能阻碍
两颗真心的结合，
那种变化无常的情不是真情，
那种见异思迁的爱不是真爱。
噢，不！爱情是亘古长明的灯塔，

在狂风暴雨中从不动摇；
爱情是指引迷舟的明星，
其高度虽可测但价值却难估量。
真爱并不受时光的愚弄，
纵然朱唇红颜逃不过岁月的侵蚀；
真爱虽短暂，却至死不渝，持之以恒直到天荒地老。
倘若我所说的皆是谬论，
那就当我未曾写此诗，世上也无人真正爱过。

审校员：乔婷

审校时间:2020.3.15

五、参考译文

两情若久长，
何虑万重山。
时变景迁见异，此情何以堪？
不如海上灯塔，淼淼烟波孤立，
独傲千叠浪。
更不比北斗，千帆望星光。
真情处，
生死无，人久长。
无意遑论，红杏春色一枕霜。
时光日月浮生，却有真情终老，
不变胜无常。
我言若虚谬，人与诗皆亡。

第四节　汉译英翻译实务

一、原文

1月底，东京的日本青少年育成协会给暴发新型冠状病毒肺炎疫情的中国湖北省捐赠的一批口罩和温度计在中国社交媒体上引发了热议。

这是因为每个箱子上都写着一句有力的诗句："山川异域，风月同天"。除了真心的关怀和文雅的语言外，这句诗也彰显了中日两国文化交流史上的一个重要时刻。这句诗出自7世纪日本长屋亲王的佛诗《绣袈裟衣缘》，长屋亲王是日本奈良时期（710—794）的一位政治家。

如题所示，这首佛诗被绣在长屋亲王命人制作的1000件袈裟上，送往中国唐朝，这是他邀请中国僧人来日本的一份诚意。这首诗也被收录进了现存最大的唐诗集《全唐诗》。

二、学生译文初稿

At the end of January, a batch of masks and thermometers donated by the Japan Youth Development Association in Tokyo to Hubei province in China, where a new coronavirus pneumonia outbreak is taking place, sparked a heated debate on Chinese social media.

This is because on each box is written a powerful verse: “United by Emotion.” .

In addition to the sincere care and gentle language, the poem also highlights an important moment in the history of cultural exchanges between China and Japan.

The poem is from the 7th century Buddhist poem “Embroidering on Kasaya for Good Karma” by prince Nagaya, a politician from the nara period（710–794).

As the title indicates, the Buddhist poem was embroidered on 1000 cassocks made by the prince Nagaya and sent to China’s Tang Dynasty as a gesture of his sincerity in inviting Chinese monks to Japan. The poem has also been included in the largest extant collection of Tang poems – “Complete Poetry of the Tang” .

——译员：张云燕

三、学生译文修改稿

At the end of January, a batch of masks and thermometers donated by the Japan Youth Development Association in Tokyo to Hubei province in China, where a new coronavirus pneumonia outbreak is taking place, sparked a heated debate on Chinese social media.

删除[乔]: hubei

This is because on each box there is written a powerful verse: " Lands apart, sky shared ".

删除[乔]: United by Emotion

In addition to the sincere care and elegant language, the poem also highlights an important moment in the history of cultural exchanges between China and Japan.

删除[乔]:

删除[乔]: gentle

The poem is from the 7th century Buddhist poem " Embroidery on Kasaya for Good Karma" by prince Nagaya, a politician from the Nara period (710-794) in Japan.
As the title indicates, the Buddhist poem was embroidered on 1,000 pieces of robes made by the prince Nagaya and sent to China in Tang Dynasty as a gesture of his sincerity in inviting Chinese monks to Japan. This poem has also been included in the largest extant collection of Tang poems–"Quan Tang Poems".

删除[乔]: buddhist

删除[乔]: Embroidering

删除[乔]: nara

删除[乔]: buddhist

删除[乔]: cassocks

删除[乔]: 's

删除[A]: The

删除[A]: Complete Poetry of the Tang

审校员：乔婷

审校时间：2020.3.15

四、学生译文终稿

At the end of January, a batch of masks and thermometers donated by the Japan Youth Development Association in Tokyo to Hubei province in China, where a new coronavirus pneumonia outbreak is taking place, sparked a heated debate on Chinese social media.

This is because on each box there is written a powerful verse: “ Lands apart, sky shared” .

In addition to the sincere care and elegant language, the poem also highlights an important moment in the history of cultural exchanges between China and Japan.

The poem is from the 7th century Buddhist poem “Embroidery on Kasaya for Good Karma” by prince Nagaya, a politician from the Nara period（710–794）in Japan.

As the title indicates, the Buddhist poem was embroidered on 1,000 pieces of robes made by the prince Nagaya and sent to China in Tang Dynasty as a gesture of his sincerity in inviting Chinese monks to Japan. This poem has also been included in the largest extant collection of Tang poems – “Quan Tang Poems” .

审校员：乔婷

审校时间：2020.3.15

五、参考译文

In late January, a donation of masks and thermometers from the Japan Youth Development Association in Tokyo to the coronavirus-stricken Hubei Province caused a stir on Chinese social media.

This was because of the powerful poetic message written on each box: “山川异域，风月同天。” Besides the heartfelt regard and the elegant language, the quote also alluded a significant moment in the history of cultural exchange between the two countries. The line comes from a seventh century Buddhist hymn by Prince Nagaya, a politician from the Nara period（710–794）of Japan, titled “Embroidered on Kasaya Robes for Good Karma”.

As the title suggests, the hymn was embroidered on 1,000 Buddhist robes which Prince Nagaya had made and sent to the Tang court in China, part of his invitation for Chinese Buddhist monks to visit Japan. The poem was also included in the Complete Tang Poems, the largest existing collection of Tang poetry.

第五节　翻译实务评析

一、词法分析

文化文本是文化互动的信息载体，主题涵盖文学、艺术、哲学、礼仪习俗等，体裁呈多样化特征。用词讲究“雅”，常引用诗词体现其文本韵味。例如，在原文（汉译英）中，“山川异域，风月同天”就引用了诗词，译者将其译为“Lands apart, sky shared”，保留了原文的结构，且准确传达了原文的信息。其次，文化翻译中涉及大量的典籍名称的翻译，可采取音译策略。例如，在原文（汉译英）中，《全唐诗》被译为“Quan Tang Poems”。此外，文化翻译，尤其诗歌中常出现单词简写的情况。例如，在原文（英译汉）中，第五行的“O”就是对语气词“Oh”的简写，再如“Love's not Time's fool”一句中，显然“Love's”就是对“Love is”的简写，这与诗歌的文本特征是分不开的。

二、句法分析

诗歌翻译讲求押韵。例如，在原文（英译汉）中，一三句的“minds”和“finds”押韵、二四句的“love”和“remove”押韵，这种隔行押韵的例子在诗歌翻译中比比皆是。而译者在翻译过程中并没有刻意追求文本的形式对应，而是着眼于语言的功能对等，对原文进行了拆分重组。例如，译者将原文（英译汉）中原本不押韵的三四两句进行重组，译成对仗工整的中文。此外，文化翻译句子灵活，长短不一。例如，原文（汉译英）中第一段是一个长句，而第二段则是一个短句，这体现了英文长短句糅杂的特征。而句子结构的灵活性在诗歌翻译中表现的尤为突出，且有些句子不符合常规的语法结构，原文中“Which alters when it alteration finds”就是一个不规则句。

三、语篇分析

文化文本的逻辑性并不强，语篇简洁凝练，篇幅较短。例如，原文（英译汉）是一首十四行诗，整体衔接紧凑、浑然一体。译者在翻译时考虑到原文的语篇特征，译文同样简洁凝练、生动传神。文化文本多属于信息类文本，多为了陈述某一特定时期的文化、历史、文学等，这也是其语言篇幅短小的原因之一，旨在清楚传递信息。例如，原文（汉译英）旨在交代《绣袈裟衣缘》一诗的历史背景，向目的语读者传递中国特色文化。综上可见，文化文本具有简洁凝练的语篇特征。

【课外拓展】

选取一首英文诗歌，进行朗诵。

文献参考

[1]郭建中．翻译中的文化因素:异化与归化[J]．上海外国语大学学报,1998(02):13-20.

[2]黄忠廉．翻译项目管理[M]．北京:国防工业出版社,2014.

[3]王宏印．中国文化典籍翻译[M]．北京:外语教学与研究出版社.

[4]王宁．全球化时代的文化研究和翻译研究[J]．中国翻译,2000(01):10-14.

[5]徐丹．文化融合中的语言翻译问题[J]．中国翻译,1998(03):3-6.

[6]许建平,张荣曦．跨文化翻译中的异化与归化问题[J]．中国翻译,2002(05):38-41.

[7]谢建平．文化翻译与文化“传真”[J]．中国翻译,2001(05):20-23.

第三章　外事翻译

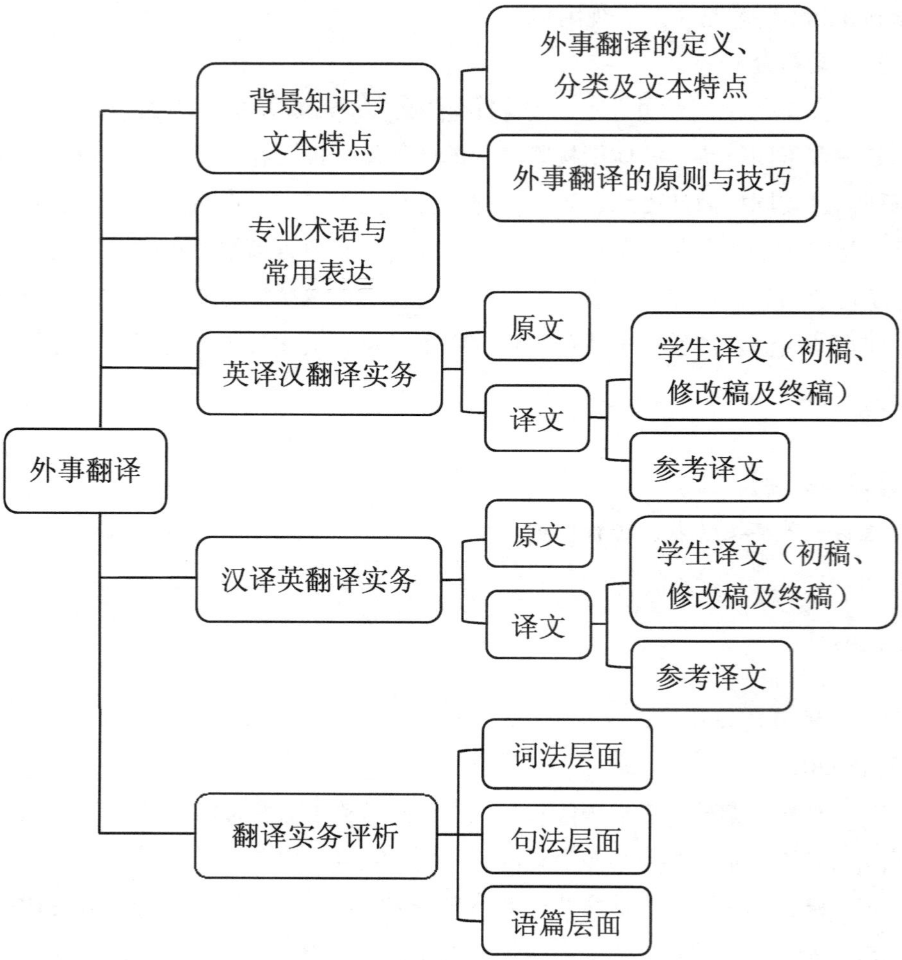
外事翻译
背景知识与文本特点
外事翻译的定义、分类及文本特点
外事翻译的原则与技巧
专业术语与常用表达
英译汉翻译实务
原文
译文
学生译文（初稿、修改稿及终稿）
参考译文
汉译英翻译实务
原文
译文
学生译文（初稿、修改稿及终稿）
参考译文
翻译实务评析
词法层面
句法层面
语篇层面

第一节　背景知识与文本特点

一、外事翻译定义、分类及文本特点

外事为“对外交流”，交流则包含语言内容的信息转换与传递，也就是翻译的本质。因此，外事是翻译的内涵之一，翻译则是外事的具体表现形式。根据不同角度，外事翻译可分为以下几类：第一，“母语—外语”翻译与“外语—母语”翻译；第二，由于翻译处理方式的不同，外事翻译可分为全译、节译、摘译、编译和译述；第三，外事笔译与外事口译。外事类文本特征显著，特点鲜明。首先，外事类文本具有较强的政治性和政策性，翻译内容多涉及国家政策、方针以及相关政治、历史事件的观点和主张，它代表着国家的立场和观点；其次，语言方面要求严谨且具有一定的分寸感。由于外事类文本内容的特殊性，需忠实向读者传达原文内容，并让读者准确理解其含义是外事翻译的主要目的。因此，在翻译的过程中需格外注重言语的严谨性和分寸感；再者，外事翻译也有较强的时效性。外事翻译的内容通常会涉及最近发生的国内外时事，因此，时间性很强，在访问、会面、谈判等重要场合进行即时翻译时，不仅要对内容中所涉及的各类事件及其背景有所了解，而且要在有限的时间内对原文所提到的事件及针对该事件的立场、观点做出恰当的翻译，这对译员来说是一项很大的挑战；最后，外事翻译具备较强的保密性，主要是因为外事类文本内容的特殊性，其文本内容与国家重要机密以及国家利益息息相关，甚至会代表整个国家的立场。因此，外事类文本的翻译具有较高的机密性。

二、外事翻译的原则与技巧

首先，就翻译原则而言，外事类文本的翻译由于其文本内容的特殊性和重要性，应遵循以下几类原则，即政治性、时代性、时效性、灵活性、准确性等；其次，多种翻译技巧供译员选择，如：（1）运用归化和异化策略，归化就是异质文化的本土表达，使译文读起来易懂、舒服；异化则指忠实转达译出语的文化特色。异化和归化两种译法各有各的特点，需要译者视目的语读者的需要及翻译目的而定，从而让译文更加准确无误，能够吸引读者的眼球且使译文读起来更加顺畅。（2）运用注释法，由于外事类文本的内容往往涉及一些政治术语，而这些政治术语常常涉及一些背景知识，更重要的是这些术语可能会涉及国家层面的信息传递。因此，单纯地直译并不能使读者清晰地理解其含义，而且译文必须准确、完整，这时就需要译者使用注释法。(3) 转换译法，译者可对原句中的词类、句型和语态等进行转换，从而使译文更加清晰、明确。

第二节　专业术语与常用表达

ST	TT
1.亚欧会议	ASEM(Asia-Europe Meeting)
2.东盟(即东南亚国家联盟)	ASEAN(Association of Southeast Asian Nations)
3东亚共同体	EAC(East Asian Community)
4.大规模杀伤性武器	WMD(Weapons of Mass Destruction)
5.国内生产总值	GDP(Gross Domestic Product)
6.《不扩散核武器条约》	NPT(Nonproliferation Treaty)
7.中国梦	the Chinese Dream
8.不忘初心	stay true to the mission
9.两个一百年	two centenary goals
10.新常态	new normal
11.中国制造	Made in China
12."双一流"	"Double First-Class" initiative
13.工匠精神	craftsmanship spirit
14.中国天眼:500米口径球面射电望远镜	China' Eye of Heaven: The Five-hundred-meter Aperture Spherical Telescope(FAST)
15.歼20隐形战机	J-20 stealth fighter
16.国产航母	domestically built aircraft carrier
17.国产客机	domestically produced passenger jet
18.可燃冰试采	sampling of combustible ice
19.量子卫星"墨子号"	quantum satellite"Micius"
20.北斗卫星导航系统	Beidou navigation system
21.风云四号A星卫星	Fengyun-4A satellite
22.重型运载火箭	heavy-lift carrier rocket

续表

ST	TT
23.沪港通	Shanghai-Hong Kong Stock Connect
24.深港通	Shenzhen-Hong Kong Stock Connect
25.京津冀一体化	Beijing-Tianjin-Hebei integration
26.雄安新区	Xiong'an New Area
27.自贸试验区	pilot free trade zones
28.医疗改革	medical reform
29.供给侧改革	supply side reform
30.扫脸支付	face scan payment
31.二维码支付	QR code payment
32.人工智能	artificial intelligence
33.虚拟现实	virtual reality
34.5G时代	5G era
35.点赞	give a like
36自媒体	We-Media
37.实名认证	real-name authentication
38.精准扶贫	targeted poverty reduction
39.精准医疗	precision medicine
40.利益共同体	community of shared interests
41.香港回归祖国20周年	the 20th anniversary of Hong Kong's return to China
42.轨道交通	rail traffic
43.动车	bullet train
44."一带一路"倡议	Belt and Road Initiative
45.文化自信	cultural confidence
46.新型大国关系	new model/type of major power relationship
47.海外代购	overseas purchasing agency
48.自驾游	self-driving tours
49.无现金支付	cashless payment
50反腐剧	anti-corruption TV series

第三节　英译汉翻译实务

一、原文

The second meeting of the Emergency Committee convened by the WHO Director-General under the International Health Regulations（IHR)（2005） regarding the outbreak of novel coronavirus 2019 in the People's Republic of China, took place on Thursday, 30 January 2020, from 13:30 to 18:35 Geneva time（CEST). The Committee's role is to give advice to the Director-General, who makes the final decision on the determination of a Public Health Emergency of International Concern（PHEIC). The Committee also provides public health advice or suggests formal Temporary Recommendations as appropriate.

The Committee welcomed the leadership and political commitment of the very highest levels of Chinese government, their commitment to transparency, and the efforts made to investigate and contain the current outbreak. China quickly identified the virus and shared its sequence, so that other countries could diagnose it quickly and protect themselves, which has resulted in the rapid development of diagnostic tools.

二、学生译文初稿

2020年1月30日，星期四，日内瓦时间13：30至18：35（中欧夏令时），世界卫生组织总干事根据《国际卫生条例（2005）》召开突发事件委员会第二次会议，讨论2019年中华人民共和国爆发的新型冠状病毒疫情。委员会的作用是向总干事提供咨询意见，后由总干事就确定国际关注的突发公共卫生事件做出最后决定。委员会还会酌情提供公共卫生咨询，或根据情况提出临时建议。

委员会赞许中国高层政府的领导和政治承诺，对疫情透明度的承诺，以及为调查和遏制当前疫情而做出的努力。中国迅速研究了新型冠状病毒，并分享其基因序列给其他国家，以便其他国家能够迅速诊断并采取保护措施，这也促进了诊断工具的迅速发展。

——译员：王鹏燕

三、学生译文修改稿

日内瓦时间 2020 年 1 月 30 日，星期四，下午一点三十分至六点三十五分（中欧夏令时），世界卫生组织总干事根据《国际卫生条例（2005）》召开了突发事件委员会第二次会议。会议讨论了中国爆发的 2019 新型冠状病毒疫情。该委员会的作用是向总干事提供意见以便总干事就确定国际关注的突发公共卫生事件做出最后决定。委员会还会提供公共卫生意见，或根据情况提出正式的临时建议。

委员会对中国政府最高层的领导能力、政治承诺和对疫情透明度的保证，以及为调查和控制当前疫情而做出的努力感到欣慰。中国迅速对新型冠状病毒进行了研究，并与其他国家分享了其基因序列，以便他们能够迅速诊断出该病毒并采取保护措施，这也促进了诊断工具的迅速发展。

委员会认为，只要各国采取强有力的措施，能及早发现、隔离和治疗感染者，追踪接触者，以及实行与风险相称的社会隔离措施，就有可能阻断病毒传播。值得注意的是，随着疫情的不断变化，预防和减少病毒传播的战略目标和措施也将随之改变。委员会一致认为，此次疫情符合国际关注的突发公共卫生事件标准，并提出以下建议作为临时建议发布。

删除[杨]：日内瓦时间

删除[杨]：中华人民共和国

删除[杨]：咨询

删除[杨]：，后由

删除[杨]：酌情

删除[杨]：咨询

删除[杨]：赞许

删除[杨]：高层

删除[杨]：和

删除[杨]：承诺

删除[杨]：遏制

删除[杨]：研究了

删除[杨]：给其他国家

删除[杨]：疾病

删除[杨]：患者

删除[杨]：局势的不断发展

删除[杨]：感染

审校：张静&杨雯

日期：2020.03.28

四、学生译文终稿

日内瓦时间2020年1月30日，星期四，下午一点三十分至六点三十五分（中欧夏令时），世界卫生组织总干事根据《国际卫生条例（2005）》召开了突发事件委员会第二次会议。会议讨论了中国爆发的2019新型冠状病毒疫情。该委员会的作用是向总干事提供意见以便总干事就确定国际关注的突发公共卫生事件做出最后决定。委员会还会提供公共卫生意见，或根据情况提出正式的临时建议。

委员会对中国政府最高层的领导能力、政治承诺和对疫情透明度的保证，以及为调查和控制当前疫情而做出的努力感到欣慰。中国迅速对新型冠状病毒进行了研究，并与其他国家分享了其基因序列，以便他们能够迅速诊断出该病毒并采取保护措施，这也促进了诊断工具的迅速发展。

审校：张静&杨雯

日期：2020.03.28

五、参考译文

世卫组织总干事根据《国际卫生条例（2005）》召集的突发事件委员会于2020年1月30日（星期四）日内瓦时间（欧洲中部时间）13:30至18:35举行会议，讨论中华人民共和国发生的2019新型冠状病毒疫情。委员会的作用是向总干事提供咨询意见，由总干事就确定是否构成国际关注的突发公共卫生事件作出最后决定。委员会还提供公共卫生咨询意见或酌情提出正式的临时建议。

对中国政府最高领导人的领导作用、政治承诺和在透明度方面的决心，以及为调查和控制当前疫情所做的努力，委员会表示欢迎。中国迅速识别了这一病毒，并分享了病毒的基因序列，促进迅速开发出诊断工具，使其他国家能够迅速作出诊断和采取防护措施。

第四节　汉译英翻译实务

一、原文

比尔·盖茨：

你好！在中国抗击新冠肺炎疫情的关键时刻，你和夫人领导的基金会慷慨解囊，你给我写信表达对中国人民的支持，我对此表示衷心的感谢。

疫情发生以后，我提出了坚定信心、同舟共济、科学防治、精准施策的总要求，我们举全国之力进行防控，采取一系列前所未有的防控和救治举措，取得了重大成效。我们坚决维护中国人民生命安全和身体健康，也坚决维护世界各国人民生命安全和身体健康，努力为全球公共卫生安全作出贡献。

我一直讲，人类是一个命运共同体。战胜关乎各国人民安危的疫病，团结合作是最有力的武器。盖茨基金会很早就加入全球抗击新冠肺炎疫情的行动，发挥了积极作用。我支持盖茨基金会同中方有关机构的合作。我也期待国际社会加强协调，为维护人类健康福祉而一起努力。

二、学生译文初稿

Hello! Mr Bill Gates, I want to express my heartfelt thanks to you and your wife for writing to me to express your support to the Chinese people and donations at a critical moment in fighting against the COVID−19 in China.

After the outbreak, I have proposed the general requirements of strengthening confidence, mutual aid, scientific control, and targeted measures. We took national efforts to prevent and control, and adopted a series of unprecedented prevention and control and rescue measures, which have achieved significant results. We resolutely safeguard the life safety and physical health of the Chinese people and other people all over the world, and spare no efforts to contribute to global public health security.

I have been saying that human beings are a community of shared future. Solidarity and cooperation are the most powerful weapons to overcome epidemics that are related to the safety of people of all countries. The Gates Foundation joined the global effort to combat the COVID−19 early and has played an active role in it. I support the cooperation between the Gates Foundation and relevant Chinese institutions. I also expect the international community to strengthen coordination and work together to safeguard human health and well−being.

——译员：陈春

三、学生译文修改稿

汉译英

Hello! Mr. Bill Gates, I want to express my heartfelt thanks to you and your wife's foundation for writing to me to express your support to the Chinese people and generous donations at a critical moment in fighting against the COVID-19 in China.

删除[A]: Mr

After the outbreak, I put forward the general requirements of firm confidence, mutual aid, scientific control, and precise measures. We have achieved significant results because we took national efforts to prevent and control, and adopted a series of unprecedented prevention and control and rescue measures, We resolutely safeguard the life health of the Chinese people and other people all over the world, and strive to contribute to global public health security.

删除[A]: have proposed the

删除[A]: strengthening

删除[A]: targeted

删除[A]: which have achieved significant results.

删除[乔]: safety and physical

删除[A]: spare no efforts

I have always said that human beings are a community of shared future. Solidarity and cooperation are the most powerful weapons to overcome epidemics that are related to the safety of people of all countries. The Gates Foundation has joined the global effort to combat the COVID-19 early and has played an active role in it. I support the cooperation between the Gates Foundation and relevant Chinese institutions. I also look forward to strengthening coordination among the international community and work together to safeguard human health and well-being.

删除[A]: been

删除[A]: saying

删除[A]: the international community to strengthen

审校员：何丽霞

审校时间：2020.03.28

四、学生译文终稿

Hello! Mr. Bill Gates, I want to express my heartfelt thanks to you and your wife's foundation for writing to me to express your support to the Chinese people and generous donations at a critical moment in fighting against the COVID-19 in China.

After the outbreak, I put forward the general requirements of firm confidence, mutual aid, scientific control, and precise measures. We have achieved significant results because we took national efforts to prevent and control, and adopted a series of unprecedented prevention and control and rescue measures, We resolutely safeguard the life health of the Chinese people and other people all over the world, and strive to contribute to global public health security.

I have always said that human beings are a community of shared future. Solidarity and cooperation are the most powerful weapons to overcome epidemics that are related to the safety of people of all countries. The Gates Foundation has joined the global effort to combat the COVID-19 early and has played an active role in it. I support the cooperation between the Gates Foundation and relevant Chinese institutions. I also look forward to strengthening coordination among the international community and work together to safeguard human health and well-being.

审校员：何丽霞

审校时间：2020.03.28

五、参考译文

It was nice to receive your letter. Now is a critical moment in China's fight against the novel coronavirus disease（COVID-19). I deeply appreciate the act of generosity of the Bill & Melinda Gates Foundation and your letter of solidarity to the Chinese people at such an important moment.

Since the outbreak began, I have called for confidence, unity, science-based approach and targeted response as guidelines for China's epidemic control efforts. We have rallied the whole nation and adopted a string of unprecedented measures to contain and mitigate the epidemic and treat the sick. These extraordinary measures are delivering substantial results. We are resolute in protecting the life and health of the people of China, and of all countries around the world. We are determined to do our part to uphold global public health security.

As I often say, mankind is a community with a shared future. To prevail over a disease that threatens all, unity and cooperation is the most powerful weapon. The Foundation has been quick in joining the global action and has played an active role in the global response against the outbreak. I support your cooperation with relevant Chinese institutions, and look forward to enhanced coordination and concerted efforts in the international community for the sake of health and well-being of all.

第五节　翻译实务评析

一、词法分析

译者对于词汇的选择能够直观呈现出其语言功底。这一点，在外事文本翻译中尤为明显。“词性转换”是译者词法处理技巧的体现。例如：原文（英译汉）第一段中“outbreak”为名词词性，但在译文中，译者根据上下文语境及行文需求，将其处理为动词“爆发”，使其更为符合汉语的表达习惯。此外，汉语常用“四字格”来体现文章的工整和语气的强烈，而英语则无此表达习惯。例如：原文（汉译英）第一段中“坚定信心、同舟共济、科学防治、精准施策”等词，译者在译文中将其统一处理为“形容词+名词”的形式，既保留原文的强调语气，又符合英语的语言风格。

二、句法分析

外事文本句式结构严谨，句子间关系紧密。例如：对原文（英译汉）第一句“The second meeting of the Emergency Committee convened by the WHO Director-General under the International Health Regulations（IHR)（2005）regarding the outbreak of novel coronavirus 2019 in the People’s Republic of China, took place on Thursday, 30 January 2020, from 13:30 to 18:35 Geneva time（CEST)”进行翻译时，学生译文对其进行了拆分整理，将时间及地点置于句首，使用拆译法对原句进行了重组，但不足之处是译者仅对原句的语序进行了调整，最终成型的译文仍然为一个较为冗长的句子，使得句意不清，而参考译文将原句分为两个短句，既不影响句意的表达，又使译文清晰明了。汉语中，句子的语态及时态变化不显著，而英语则恰恰相反。例如：原文（汉译英）中没有明显的时态变换，但译文中，译者综合采用多种时态，来体现“疫情”发生时、发生后及当下的时间发展顺序，体现了英文的语言特色。

三、语篇分析

外事文本政治性强、内容明晰准确、结构严谨。译者在对译文进行排篇布局时绝不可模糊外事文本的文体特征。为了使译文读者与原文读者的阅读效果等同，译者对于某些表示衔接关系的词及各类代词的使用都以遵从原文为准则，即原文中有此类词，则译文中也有所体现，若原文中没有体现出明显的衔接手段，译文中也不过多进行增译。总之，保证真实性与连贯性是译者对外事文本语篇规划时需率先遵从的原则。

【课外拓展】

请选取近一年内中国重要的外事场合，与你的团队进行模拟同传练习。

文献参考

[1]范武邱,信萧萧．外交翻译中的口吻传译[J]．上海翻译,2017(06):16-20+42+93.

[2]黄忠廉,李亚舒．论翻译策略系统[J]．上海科技翻译,2003(04):10-13+25.

[3]黄忠廉．变译全译:一对新的翻译范畴[J]．上海科技翻译,2002(03):5-7.

[4]黄忠廉．翻译项目管理[M]．北京:国防工业出版社,2014.

[5]李德超．TAPs翻译过程研究二十年:回顾与展望[J]．中国翻译,2005(01):29-34.

[6]涂和平．外事翻译的政治性和时代性[J]．上海翻译,2005(03):37-39.

[7]屠国元,朱献珑．译者主体性:阐释学的阐释[J]．中国翻译,2003(06):10-16.

[8]王蕾．英语构词转类法与英汉翻译词汇转译法[J]．上海翻译,2006(03):24-27.

[9]袁晓宁．也谈E/C和C/E翻译单位的确定[J]．中国翻译,2006(03):43-46.

第四章　经济翻译

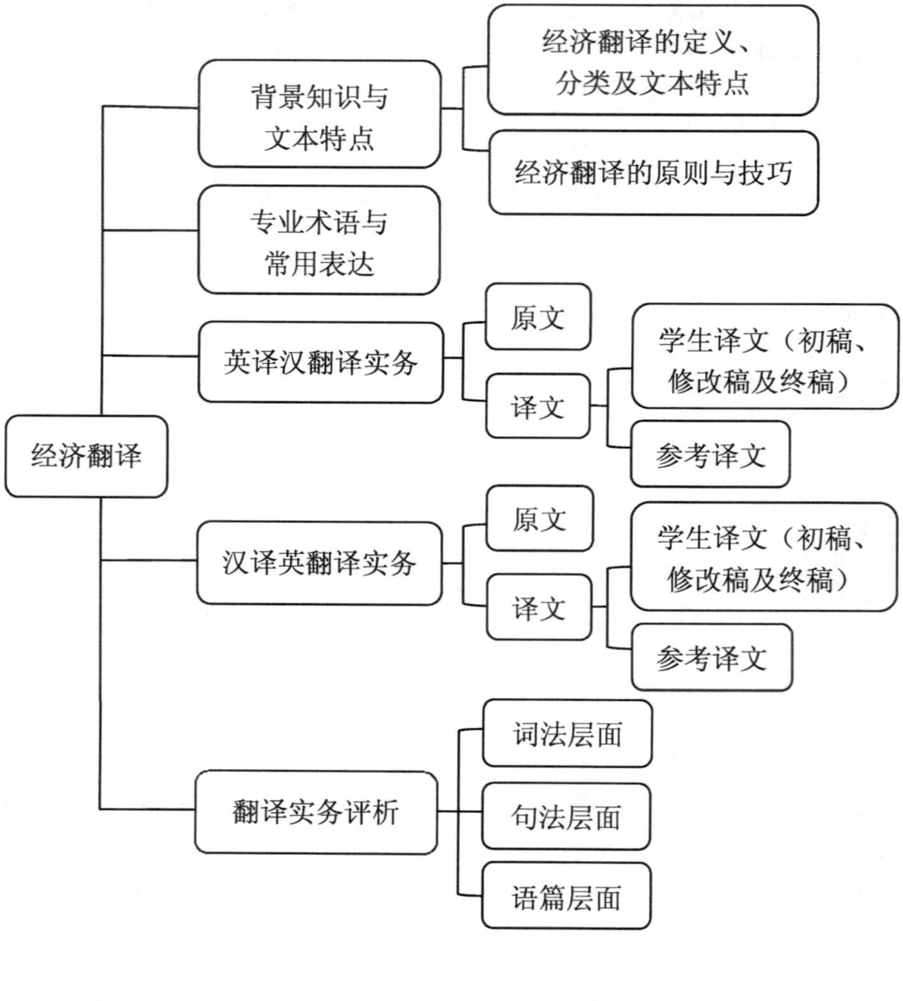
经济翻译
背景知识与文本特点
经济翻译的定义、分类及文本特点
经济翻译的原则与技巧
专业术语与常用表达
英译汉翻译实务
原文
译文
学生译文（初稿、修改稿及终稿）
参考译文
汉译英翻译实务
原文
译文
学生译文（初稿、修改稿及终稿）
参考译文
翻译实务评析
词法层面
句法层面
语篇层面

第一节　背景知识与文本特点

一、经济翻译的定义、分类及文本特点

经济（economic）一词源于希腊语，意指“管理一个家庭的人”，人类经济活动的本质就是创造、转化、实现价值。经济文本涉及的领域可细分为：普通经济、政治经济、微观经济、宏观经济、要素经济、数量经济、信息经济、制度经济、区域经济、行业经济、管理经济和国际经济等。对于任何行业的翻译而言，专业性和准确性都是最基本的要求，经济类翻译同样也不例外。翻译这类资料时，必须保证经济类专业术语的准确，避免出现低级错误。

二、翻译的原则和技巧

经济翻译首先要忠实于原文，表达要准确严谨、统一规范。可以采用顺译、转换、增补、切分或删减信息等翻译方法，在翻译时不可只局限于一种译法，要根据文本特征，灵活运用不同策略处理文本。同时，在翻译时要注意以下几个方面：

1.专业词汇和术语的翻译

经济翻译在涉及商务活动时大量使用专业词汇和专业术语。因此，做这类翻译首先要有专业词汇和术语知识的储备。有些词汇在商务翻译中具有特殊的意义，在翻译过程中也要注重查阅专业辞典，保证准确性。与此同时，经济翻译涉及的领域非常广，在翻译不同方面的资料时，要多查阅文献资料，辞典著作，多向行业内人士请教，以求得译文的严谨规范。

2.语言的简洁性和逻辑的严密性

语言的简洁一般是指在商务类信函中，语句大多使用简单句。现代人生活节奏快，用简洁的语言阐述清楚一件事，更能提高办事的效率。同时，陈述事情时要层次分明，逻辑清晰，避免内容含糊不清，在交流过程中使人误解，造成经济上的损失。

3.数字的翻译

经济类文本离不开数字、百分数和倍数。英语数字表达与汉语表达方式不同，译为汉语时需要换算成对应的单位数值。如果翻译有误，严重时可能会造成很大的经济损失。因此，对于数字的表达，平时一定要多练习，熟能生巧，多查阅资料，尤其数字翻译中涉及的套话术语要翻译精确。

4.被动语态的翻译

经济类文本多用被动语态客观的陈述事实，掌握被动语态的翻译，会让读者更易理解原文内容。在将句子译成汉语时，可将被动变为主动语态，更符合汉语的表达习惯。

第二节 专业术语与常用表达

ST	TT
1.绝对优势	absolute advantage
2.逆向选择	adverse choice
3.选择成本	alternative cost
4.需求的弧弹性	arc elasticity of demand
5.非对称的信息	asymmetric information
6.平均成本	average cost
7.平均固定成本	average fixed cost
8.平均产品	average product
9.平均可变成本	average variable cost
10.贝塔系数	Beta
11.债券收益	bond yield
12.收支平衡图	break-even chart
13.预算线	budget line
14.捆绑销售	bundling
15.资本	capital
16.资本收益	capital gain
17.资本主义	capitalism
18.基数效用	cardinal utility
19.卡特尔	cartel
20.科布—道格拉斯生产函数	Cobb-Douglas production function
21.勾结	collision
22.比较优势	comparative advantage

续表

ST	TT
23.互补品	complements
24.成本不变行业	constant-cost industry
25.规模收益不变	constant returns to scale
26.消费者剩余	consumer surplus
27.可竞争市场	contestable market
28.契约曲线	contract curve
29.角点解	corner solution
30.需求的交叉弹性	cross elasticity of demand
31.垄断的无谓损失	dead weight loss of monopoly
32.买方垄断的无谓损失	dead weight loss of monopsony
33.成本递减行业	decreasing-cost industry
34.规模收益递减	decreasing return to scale
35.需求曲线	demand curve
36.可贷资金的需求曲线	demand curve of loanable funds
37.贴现率	discount rate
38.可分散风险	diversifiable risk
39.主导厂商	dominant firm
40.优势策略	dominant strategy
41.双头垄断	duopoly
42.经济效率	economic efficiency
43.经济利润	economic profit
44.生产的经济区域	economic region of production
45.经济资源	economic resource
46.范围经济	economies of scope
47.有效市场假说	Efficient Markets Hypothesis(EMH)
48.财富状况	endowment position
49.恩格尔曲线	Engel curve
50.均衡	equilibrium

第三节 英译汉翻译实务

一、原文

FRANKFURT — The European Central Bank took a series of unexpected and radical steps on Thursday to stimulate the sluggish Eurozone economy, including effectively paying banks to lend money.

While increasing the penalty it charges banks to store funds in its virtual vaults, as expected, the central bank surprised analysts and investors by saying it would also offer four-year loans to commercial banks under an arrangement that would pay the banks interest on money they lend to businesses and consumers.

The actions, which go well beyond what analysts predicted, are part of an increasingly urgent effort by the central bank to give the Eurozone economy a decisive shove and to head off the threat of a destructive decline in prices known as deflation.

But the moves are not without risks, taking the central bank further into the relatively uncharted territory of so-called negative interest rates.

The central bank also said it would expand its purchases of government bonds and other assets to 80 billion euros, or about $88 billion, a month from €60 billion. In another unprecedented step for the Eurozone, the central bank will also begin buying corporate bonds as part of the asset purchases.

The announcement of the moves prompted an immediate plunge in the euro against the dollar, which is good for European exporters, while stocks rose. But the unexpectedly forceful action could also be interpreted as a sign that the European Central Bank is more worried than analysts thought about the risk of deflation.

二、学生译文初稿

法兰克福——周四，欧洲央行采取了一系列出人意料的激进措施，如为银行出资让其发放贷款等，以此来刺激疲软的欧元区经济。

同时，欧洲央行还增长了银行存储基金存放在虚拟金库的罚款，这都在分析人士和投资者的意料之中。他们意料之外的是，该行表示，根据一份协议，它还会向商业银行提供为期4年的贷款，用于支付商业银行向企业和消费者发放贷款的利息。

这些举措虽然远远超出了分析人士的预期，但也是欧洲央行做出迫切努力的一部分。欧洲央行想要给欧元区经济一个决定性的推力，防止物价破坏性下跌(通货紧缩)。

即便如此，这些举措也不是没有风险，它们会将欧洲央行带入一个相对陌生的领域，即所谓的逆利率。

欧洲央行还表示，它将把每月购买政府债券和其他资产的规模从600亿欧元扩大至800亿欧元(约合880亿美元)，还将开始购买公司债券，作为资产购买计划的一部分。这是欧元区采取的又一个前所未有的举措。

这些举措宣布后，欧元兑美元汇率立即大幅下跌，这有利于欧洲出口商品；同时，股市上涨。但这些出乎意料的强力举措也可能被解读成一个信号，暗示欧洲央行比分析人员预想的更担心通货紧缩风险。

——译员：张云燕

三、学生译文修改稿

法兰克福——周四，欧洲中央银行采取了一系列出人意料的激进措施，如出钱让银行放贷，以此来刺激疲软的欧元区经济。

正如预期的那样，在加大了银行存储基金存放在虚拟金库的处罚力度的同时，欧洲央行还表示，将根据一份协议，向商业银行提供为期4年的贷款，用于支付商业银行向企业和消费者发放贷款的利息。这一举措令分析人士和投资者感到惊讶。

这些远远超出了分析人士预期的举措是欧洲央行做出迫切努力的一部分。欧洲央行试图通过该行动给欧元区经济一个决定性的推力，并防止通货紧缩而带来的物价破坏性下跌的威胁。

但这些举措存在着使央行深陷相对未知的负利率领域的风险。

欧洲央行还表示，它将把每月购买政府债券和其他资产的规模从600亿欧元扩大至800亿欧

删除[杨]：央行

删除[杨]：同时，

删除[杨]：欧洲央行还

删除[杨]：增长

删除[杨]：罚款

删除[杨]：这都在分析人士和投资者的意料之中。他们意料之外的是，

删除[杨]：该行

删除[杨]：它还会

删除[杨]：举措虽然

删除[杨]：的

删除[杨]：，但也

删除[杨]：想要

删除[杨]：（通货紧缩）

元(约合 880 亿美元)，还将开始购买公司债券，作为资产购买计划的一部分。这是欧元区采取的又一个前所未有的举措。

这些举措宣布后，欧元兑美元汇率立即大幅下跌，这有利于欧洲出口商。同时，股市上涨。但这些出乎意料的强有力举措也可能被解读成一个信号，表明欧洲央行比分析人员预想的更担心通货紧缩风险。

删除[杨]: 品

删除[杨]: ；

删除[杨]: 暗示

审校：张静&杨雯
时间：2020. 04. 18

四、学生译文终稿

法兰克福—周四，欧洲中央银行采取了一系列出乎意料的激进措施以刺激疲软的欧元区经济，例如出钱让银行放贷。

正如预期的那样，在加大了对银行将资金存储在虚拟金库的惩罚力度的同时，欧洲央行还表示，将根据一项协议规定，向商业银行提供四年期贷款，以供银行给企业和消费者支付贷款利息。这一举措令分析师和投资者感到十分意外。

这些远远超出了分析师预期的行动是该行日益紧迫的行动的一部分，旨在大力推动欧元区经济，并防止通货紧缩而带来的物价破坏性下跌的威胁。

但这些举措存在着使央行深陷相对未知的负利率领域的风险。

欧洲央行还表示，将把每月购买政府债券和其他资产的规模从600亿英镑扩大至800亿欧元（约合880亿美元)。该行还将开始购买公司债券作为资产购买的一部分。欧元区迈出了前所未有的一步。

这些举措的宣布促使欧元兑美元的汇率立即暴跌，而这有利于欧洲出口商。同时，股票上涨。但是，实际力度超出预期的行动也可以表明，欧洲央行比分析师所预期的还要担忧通货紧缩风险。

审校员：张静、杨雯
审校时间：2020.04.18

五、参考译文

法兰克福——周四，欧洲中央银行(European Central Bank)采取了一系列出人意料的激进措施，包括相当于出钱让银行放贷，以刺激疲软的欧元区经济。

正如外界预料的那样，欧洲央行加大了对银行把钱存放在其虚拟金库里的惩罚力度。与此同时，该行还表示，将按一项协议的规定，向商业银行提供四年期贷款。这些贷款将向银行支付其发放给企业和消费者的贷款产生的利息。此举令分析人士和投资者大感意外。

这些行动远远超出了分析人士此前的预期。它们是一项越来越紧迫的行动的一部分。欧洲央行试图通过该行动大力提振欧元区经济，并防止出现物价的破坏性下跌，即通货紧缩。

但这些举措并非没有风险。它们会让欧洲央行在所谓的负利率这个相对而言属于未知的领域陷得更深。

欧洲央行还表示将把每月购买政府债券和其他资产的规模从600亿欧元扩大到800亿欧元。该行还将开始购买企业债券，将其作为资产购买行动的一部分。对欧元区来说，这又是一项史无前例的举动。

这些举措的宣布促使欧元兑美元汇率立即大幅下跌。而这对欧洲出口商有利。与此同时，股市上涨。但力度超出预期的行动也可能会被当作一个迹象，表明欧洲央行比分析人士以为的更担心通货紧缩风险。

第四节 汉译英翻译实务

一、原文

中国近期经济、金融发展状况。

中国的改革开放和现代化建设取得了举世瞩目的成就，综合国力明显增强。近十几年来，中国年平均GDP增长保持在9%以上，明显高于世界平均增长率。特别是在1997年发生亚洲金融危机以及近期世界经济增长前景不确定的情况下，中国政府通过实行积极的财政政和稳健的货币政策，扩大内需，避免了经济增长的大起落，保持了经济的持续快速健康发展。

2003年以来，中国经济保持了良好发展势头，一季度经济增长显著加快，国内生产总值同比增长9.9%，2001年至2002年期间中国出现了轻微的通货紧缩，2002年的消费物价增长为负0.4%，20年居民消费价格总水平出现了自2001年11月份以来的首次上涨，1–5月居民消费物价指数同比上涨0.6%，扭转了近两年来物价持续下降的局面。

二、学生译文初稿

China's recent economic and financial development

China has made remarkable achievements in its reform, opening up and modernization drive, and its overall national strength has significantly increased. Over the past decade, China's annual average GDP growth has remained above 9%, significantly higher than the world's average growth rate. In particular, when the Asian financial crisis occurred in 1997 and the world economic growth prospects were uncertain recently, the Chinese government, through the implementation of a positive fiscal policy and a sound monetary policy, expanded domestic demand, avoided the big ups and downs of economic growth, and maintained the sustained, rapid and healthy development of the economy.

Since 2003, China's economy has maintained a good momentum of development. In the first quarter, economic growth accelerated significantly, with GDP increasing by 9.9% year-on-year. During the period of 2001 to 2002, China experienced slight deflation, the consumer price growth was minus 0.4% in 2002. In 20 years, the general level of consumer price rose for the first time since November 2001. In the first five months of the consumer price index rose 0.6%, reversing the declining prices in the past two years.

——译员：牛婷

三、学生译文修改稿

China's recent economic and financial development

China has made remarkable achievements in its reform, opening up and modernization construction, and its overall national strength has significantly enhanced. Over the past decade, China's rate of annual average GDP growth kept more than has remained above 9%, obviously higher than the world's average growth rate. Especially in 1997, under the situation of the Asian financial crisis and the world economic

删除[乔]: modernization

删除[乔]: drive

删除[乔]: increased

删除[乔]: significantly

growth prospects were uncertain recently, the Chinese government take positive fiscal policy and a prudent monetary policy to expand domestic demand and avoid major fluctuations in economic growth, and remaining the continuous growth in a healthy way.

删除[乔]: , through the implementation of a positive fiscal policy and a sound monetary policy, expanded domestic demand, avoided the big ups and downs of economic growth, and maintained the sustained, rapid and healthy development of the economy.

Since 2003, China's economy has maintained a good momentum of development. In the first quarter, economic growth accelerated significantly, with GDP increased by 9.9% year-on-year. During the period of 2001 to 2002, China appeared a slight deflation, the consumer price growth was minus 0.4% in 2002. In 20 years, the general level of consumer price rose for the first time since November 2001. In the first five months of this year, the consumer price index increased by 0.6% over the same period of last year, reversing the declining prices in the past two years.

删除[乔]: increasing

删除[乔]: experienced

删除[乔]: rose

审校员：乔婷

审校时间：2020.4.18

四、学生译文终稿

China's recent economic and financial development

China has made remarkable achievements in its reform, opening up and modernization construction, and its overall national strength has significantly enhanced. Over the past decade, China's rate of annual average GDP growth kept more than 9%, obviously higher than the world's average growth rate. Especially in 1997, under the situation of the Asian financial crisis and the world economic growth prospects were uncertain recently, the Chinese government take positive fiscal policy and a prudent monetary policy to expand domestic demand and avoid major fluctuations in economic growth, and remaining the continuous growth in a healthy way.

Since 2003, China's economy has maintained a good momentum of development. In the first quarter, economic growth accelerated significantly, with GDP increased by 9.9% year-on-year. During the period of 2001 to 2002, China appeared a slight deflation, the consumer price growth was minus 0.4% in 2002. In 20 years, the general level of consumer price rose for the first time since November 2001. In the first five months of this year, the consumer price index increased by 0.6% over the same period of last year, reversing the declining prices in the past two years.

审校员：乔婷

审校时间：2020.4.18

五、参考译文

Recent Economic and Financial Performance in China

Great achievements have been made in China's reform, opening-up and modernization drive the outside world which has caught the attention of the world. As a result, the total national strength of China has been greatly enhanced. Over the past decades, the national GDP has been above 9%, which is considerably higher than the world's average. Even with the impact of the Asian financial crisis in 1997 and of the recent uncertainty in the world economic outlook, China has been able to achieve a rapid, healthy and steady economic growth rather than suffer from drastic economic downturns. This was attributed to the implementation of the pro-active fiscal policy and the sound monetary policy to stimulate domestic demand.

Since 2003, the momentum of sound economic development has continued, with the GDP growth in the first quartet increasing by 9.9%. A slight deflation occurred in China during the period of 2001-2002. The consumer price index（CPI）was at -0.4% in 2002. Since the beginning of this year, however, it has registered its first positive turn since November 2001. In the first five months of this year, the CPI increase by 0.6% over the same period of last year, curbing the downward trend in the past two years.

第五节　翻译实务评析

一、词法分析

对译者而言，掌握经济文本的专业词汇和术语至关重要。例如：GDP、CPI等专业术语的正确运用体现了译者充分的译前准备以及丰富知识储备。其次，原文（汉译英）的标题“中国近期经济、金融发展状况”中，运用了省译法，将“发展状况”仅译为“development”一词，体现了经济文本用词简洁精炼的特点。此外，英语词汇的涵义较为广泛，词义对上下文的依赖性较大，独立性较小。而汉语词汇的涵义范围较狭窄，词义更为精确、固定、严谨，对上下文的依赖性较小，具有较强的独立性。例如：原文（英译汉）中，出现了一词多义的现象：“举措”一词可对应“steps”“actions”“moves”等词。

二、句法分析

经济双语文本中多见长难句。译者在翻译过程中应采用恰当的翻译技巧，划分句子结构，尽量让译文更加直白明了。例如：原文（汉译英）中，第二段共两个句子，但都为长难句，译者对原句结构进行了划分重组，分别译为五个短句，更为直观地表明了句子之间的逻辑关系，方便读者理解。此外，原文（英译汉）中，首段采用直译和顺译相结合的翻译方法，将时间状语“周四”提前，以贴近汉语的行文习惯，将语序转化为译文读者所熟知的方式，为译文读者扫清了阅读障碍，进一步体现了译者采用归化的翻译策略，更多地站在读者的立场上进行思考。例如：原文（英译汉）第二、三段采用拆译和逆译的翻译技巧，在具体翻译实践中合理整合语序，将语言转化成译文读者所熟悉的表达方式，进一步方便译文读者接收信息，译者还采用具体化的技巧，形象地译出了汉语的风范，值得学习与借鉴。

三、语篇分析

经济文本语言的简洁性和逻辑的严密性决定了语篇的特殊性。经济文本涉及面广且类型多样，文本措辞严密、逻辑性强、结构缜密、行文规范。例如：原文（英译汉）第六段出现“这些举措”用来指代上文中所提及的各种举措，增强了上下文的衔接，用词严谨凝练。此外，原文（英译汉）第四、五段恰当运用代词，省略一些重复出现的词语，保留了原文简洁的语言特征。

【课外拓展】

请选取财经新闻报道，进行模拟交传练习，注意其中的数字翻译。

文献参考

[1]鲍文．商务英汉/汉英翻译宏观策略研究[J]．解放军外国语学院学报，2015,38(05):20-25.

[2]鲍文,梁芸．理论、实践与教学:中国商务英语翻译研究20年[J]．中国翻译,2019,40(02):111-119.

[3]黄忠廉．翻译项目管理[M]．北京:国防工业出版社,2014.

[4]蒋阳建．商务翻译项目化教学设计[J]．上海翻译,2014(03):48-51.

[5]马会娟．论商务文本翻译标准的多元化[J]．中国翻译,2005(03):81-84.

[6]苏雯超,李德凤,何元建．商务翻译的内涵与外延[J]．中国科技翻译,2016,29(01):26-28+21.

[7]徐珺,肖海燕．基于批评体裁分析(CGA)的商务翻译研究[J]．中国外语,2016,13(04):20-28.

[8]王立非,李琳．我国商务英语研究十年现状分析(2002-2011)[J]．外语界,2013(04):2-10.

[9]王森林,肖水来．商务英语翻译[M],武汉:武汉大学出版社,2013.

第五章　教育翻译

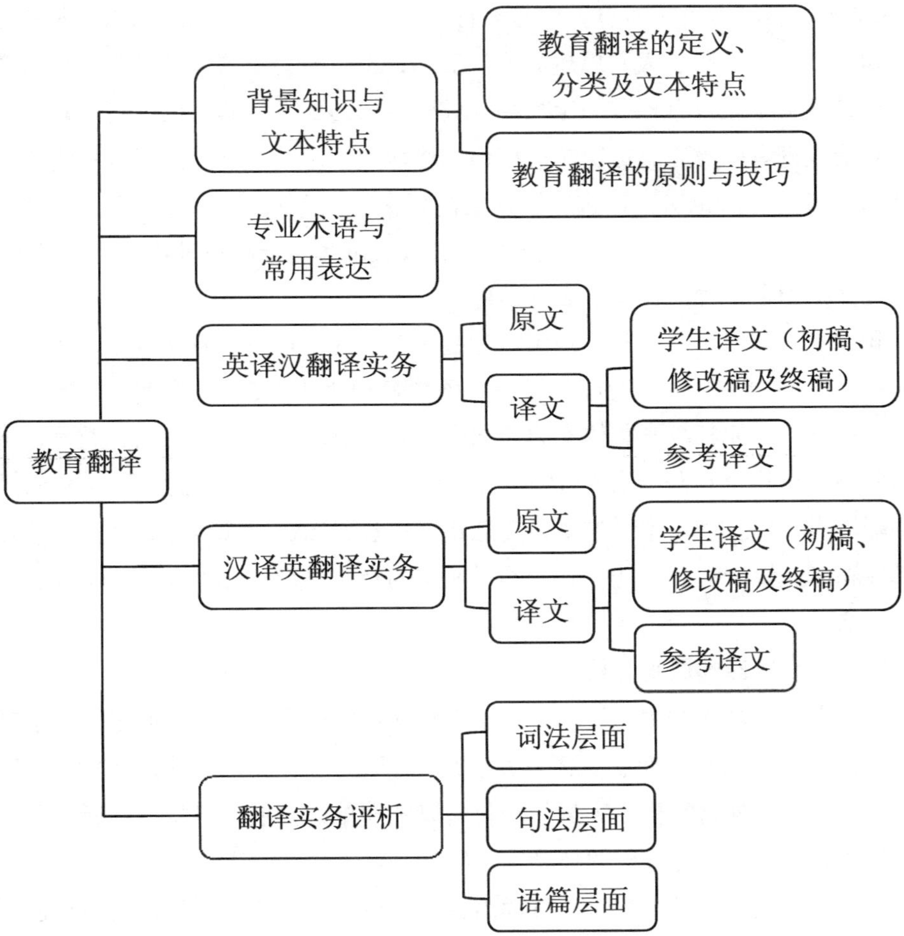
教育翻译
背景知识与文本特点
教育翻译的定义、分类及文本特点
教育翻译的原则与技巧
专业术语与常用表达
英译汉翻译实务
原文
译文
学生译文（初稿、修改稿及终稿）
参考译文
汉译英翻译实务
原文
译文
学生译文（初稿、修改稿及终稿）
参考译文
翻译实务评析
词法层面
句法层面
语篇层面

第一节 背景知识与文本特点

一、教育翻译定义、分类及文本特点

《中国大百科全书·教育》中对教育的定义如下："从广义上来说，凡是增进人们知识和技能，影响人们思想品德的活动，都是教育。狭义的教育主要指学校教育，其涵义是教育者根据一定社会（或阶级）的要求，有目的、有计划、有组织地对受教育者的身心施加影响，把他们培养成一定社会（或阶级）所需要的人的活动。"《辞海》也对翻译进行了简明的释义："翻译，把一种语言文字的意义用另一种语言文字表达出来。"顾名思义，教育翻译是指将一种语言的教育词汇、句子或文本用另一种语言文字表达出来。

我国一直致力于打造教育强国。近些年来，为了进一步发展教育，实现教育现代化，中共中央、国务院印发了《中国教育现代化2035》，为教育领域设定了教育发展方向，使其教育总体实力和国际影响力显著增强。一方面，教育文本涉及的领域十分广泛，包括各个学科，各个行业，可谓集百家之荟萃。另一方面，教育翻译属于信息型文本，主要是传达相关信息、知识、观点等，其文本特点是逻辑性和专业性较强。因此，教育翻译文本的特性决定了其内容的真实性、规范性和简洁性。

二、教育翻译的原则与技巧

教育文本的翻译原则与技巧是基于教育文本特征及翻译目的而定。鉴于教育类文本涉及词汇比较专业、文体正式、用词规范、严谨、引经据典的内容较多、多用名词以及名词化结构、大量使用长句以及简单的扩展句等特点，所以此类文本的翻译要充分考虑译入语的环境。

首先，在翻译教育文本时，目标语言文体应相对正式，同时还要注意遵循汉语的表达习惯。具体来说，句子不应过长以符合目标读者的阅读习惯。其次，基于教育文本自身的词汇、语法及句法特点，分句翻译、词性转换、逆序翻译等多种翻译策略也需灵活应用。此外，译者在翻译过程中要避免翻译策略单一。最后，由于教育文本多以政府文件、学术论文的形式为主，教育文本翻译应更多注重译文的严谨性和逻辑性。

总体来说，只有清晰把握原文本信息、文本特征、语篇逻辑关系等，才能准确无误地将原语转换为目的语，保证读者获取到基本无损的信息。也就是说，教育翻译文本的焦点应该在于内容而非形式，翻译时应以简洁明了的语言传递与原文相同的概念和信息，秉承目的性原则、忠实性原则和可读性原则进行翻译。

第二节 专业术语与常用表达

ST	TT
1.学时	credit hour
2.母校	Alma Mater
3.科举制度	imperial civil examination
4.在线直播	live streaming
5.文科院校	college of arts
6.师范大学	normal/teachers university
7.就业创业	employment and entrepreneurship
8.勤工助学	work-study program
9.复试	secondary examination
10.初试	qualifying examination/ preliminary exam
11.成绩全优生	straight A student
12.科教兴国战略	the strategy for invigorating China through science and education
13.学生综合能力	students' all-round abilities
14.孔子学院	Confucius Institute
15.招聘会	job fair
16.现场招聘	On-site recruiting
17.考勤	check roll
18.填鸭式教学法	cramming system; spoon-feeding pedagogy
19.留学生	overseas students
20.招生办公室	admission office
21.休学	schooling suspension
22.学术期刊	academic journals
23.在职培训;岗位培训	on-the-job training
24.开卷考试	open-book examination

续表

ST	TT
25.学历学位认证	schooling and academic degree certification
26.智力引进	introduce talents
27.重视教育	place considerable value on education
28.抄袭;剽窃	plagiarize / plagiarism
29.网络公开课	Massive Open Online Course(MOOC)
30.教学相长	men learn while they teach
31.非盈利教育机构	non–profit educational institutions
32.走读生	non–resident student
33.应届毕业生	graduating student
34.升学率	enrollment rate
35.复合型人才	interdisciplinary talent
36.学费上涨	jacked–up tuitions
37.课程表	school schedule
38.教学大纲	teaching program/ syllabus
39.替考者	surrogate exam–taker/ghost writer
40.学龄儿童	school–age children
41.文盲率	illiteracy rate
42.入学须知	information for admission
43.教育投入	input in education
44.高等教育资格框架	framework for higher education qualification
45.全日制教育	full–time education
46.应试教育	exam–oriented education
47.素质教育	all–round education
48.选修课	elective course
49.免考	exemption from examination
50.结业资格	exit qualification

第三节　英译汉翻译实务

一、原文

Most teachers have never given online teaching classes, so this is a novelty for them, too. They have to learn to speak naturally in front of a camera, use digital red pens during presentations, and keep the students engaged online via written comments — not an easy feat with young kids or teenagers.

Teachers in China have been using Alibaba's Ding Talk in order to hold live-streaming classes. This may sound easy for many people, but as teacher Jessie Xie from Chengdu told the South China Morning Post "It's not easy for some older teachers to learn how to do live-streaming courses. Yesterday one of my colleagues told me she still didn't know how to use it (even after the coaching session)."

The Ministry of Education recently released a statement decrying schools for making it mandatory for students to clock in and out at specific times of the day.

The ministry said schools shouldn't place a hard minimum on how much a student should study each day, nor should it be mandatory for students to film themselves studying for hours on end.

It also warned schools not to overwork teachers by requiring them to record every class and banned kindergartens from hosting online classes.

China's Ministry of Education said it will carefully arrange work related to gaokao, or national college entrance examinations, normally scheduled for June, to determine whether they should be postponed this year.

Officials said local governments should arrange the postponement of school open days based on the local epidemic situation.

Some schools in China are now embracing online learning as a method of teaching, as so many students have had to remain at home to minimize human to human interaction.

Online education and digital medical stocks continue to rise after posting huge gains last week amid the novel coronavirus outbreak.

Some analysts think that the self-quarantine period may later be recognized as a watershed moment, marking the start of a new era for online services – and the stocks closely tied to them.

Hong Kong-listed companies linked to online games, digital medical services, remote working and distance education are among new economy stocks that soared last week, as investors sensed a transformative moment might be at hand.

二、学生译文初稿

大多数教师从未尝试过在线授课，所以对他们来说这也是一个新鲜事物。他们要学会如何在镜头前运用数码笔进行自然的授课及演示，并通过书面批示让学生们保持在线参与——这对于小孩和青少年来说不是件容易的事。

中国的教师们使用阿里巴巴旗下的钉钉开直播课。这听起来很容易，但正如来自成都的谢杰西老师在接受《南华早报》采访时所说："对于年长的老师来说，学会如何操作直播课并不容易。昨天我的一位同事告诉我，她仍然不知道如何操作(即使在接受培训之后)。"

教育部近日发表声明，谴责了学校强制要求学生在特定时间内打卡的规定。

教育部表示，学校不应硬性规定学生每天的最低学习量，也不应强制学生拍摄长达数小时的学习视频。

另外，教育部就不应让教师超负荷工作，即要求教师录制每节课的内容对学校发出警告，同时禁止幼儿园开设线上课程。

中国教育部表示，将谨慎安排原定于6月举行的全国高考及相关工作，以确定今年的高考时间是否延期。

官员表示，地方政府应根据当地疫情防控情况安排学校开学时间的延期工作。

现在中国的一些学校已经开始采用在线授课，因为为了最大限度减少人与人之间的接触，很多学生必须待在家里。

新型冠状病毒疫情暴发后，在线教育股票和数字医疗股票继上周大幅上涨之后，还在继续上涨。

一些分析师认为，自我隔离期这段时间以后可能会成为一个分水岭，标志着在线服务新时代的开启——股票行情也与之密切相关。

香港上市公司，包括与网络游戏、数字医疗服务、远程办公和远程教育等行业相关的股票，成为上周飙升的新经济类股，因为投资者们意识到革新时刻可能近在眼前。

——译员：张胜霞

三、学生译文修改稿

大多数教师从未尝试过在线授课，所以对他们来说这也是一个新鲜事物。他们要学会如何在镜头前自然地讲话，演示时使用红色的数码笔，并通过打字发表意见让学生们保持在线参与——然而这对于小孩和青少年来说不是件容易的事。

删除[T]：运用

删除[T]：进行自然的授课及演示，

删除[T]：书面批示

删除[T]：

中国的教师们一直使用阿里巴巴旗下的应用软件钉钉开直播课。这听起来很容易，但正如来自成都的谢杰西老师在接受《南华早报》采访时所说："对于年长的老师来说，学会如何操作直播课并不容易。昨天我的一位同事告诉我，她仍然不知道如何操作(即使在接受培训之后)。"

教育部近日发表声明，谴责了学校强制要求学生在特定时间内打卡的规定。

教育部表示，学校不应硬性规定学生每天的最低学习量，也不应强制学生拍摄长达数小时的学习视频。

另外，教育部还警告学校不应增加教师的工作量，要求他们录制每节课内容的，同时禁止幼儿园开设线上课程。

删除[T]：就不应让

删除[T]：超负荷工作

删除[T]：即

删除[T]：教师

删除[T]：规定对学校发出警告

中国教育部表示，将谨慎安排原定于6月举行的全国高考及相关工作，以确定今年的高考时间是否延期。

教育部官员表示，地方政府应根据当地疫情防控情况安排学校推迟开学时间。

删除[T]：的延期工作

现在中国的一些学校已经开始采用在线授课，因为为了最大限度减少人与人之间的接触，很多学生必须呆在家里。

新型冠状病毒疫情爆发后，在线教育股票和数字医疗股票继上周大幅上涨之后，还在继续上涨。

一些分析师认为，自我隔离期这段时间以后可能会成为一个分水岭，标志着在线服务新时代的开启——股票行情也与之密切相关。

香港上市公司，包括与网络游戏、数字医疗服务、远程办公和远程教育等行业相关的股票，成为上周飙升的新经济类股，因为投资者们意识到革新时刻即将到来。

删除[T]：可能近在眼前

审校员：乔婷

审校时间：2020.4.4

设置格式[T]：缩进：左 -0.95 字符

四、学生译文终稿

大多数教师从未尝试过在线授课，所以对他们来说这也是一个新鲜事物。他们要学会在镜头前自然地讲话，演示时使用红色的数码笔，并通过打字发表意见让学生们保持在线参与——然而这对于小孩和青少年来说不是件容易的事。

中国的教师们一直使用阿里巴巴旗下的应用软件钉钉开直播课。这听起来很容易，但正如来自成都的谢杰西老师在接受《南华早报》采访时所说：“对于年长的老师来说，学会如何操作直播课并不容易。昨天我的一位同事告诉我，她仍然不知道如何操作（即使在接受培训之后）。”

教育部近日发表声明，谴责了学校强制要求学生在特定时间内打卡的规定。

教育部表示，学校不应硬性规定学生每天的最低学习量，也不应强制学生连续拍摄长达数小时的学习视频。

另外，教育部还警告学校不应增加教师的工作量，要求他们录制每节课内容，同时禁止幼儿园开设线上课程。

中国教育部表示，将谨慎安排原定于6月举行的全国高考及相关工作，以确定今年的高考时间是否延期。

教育部官员表示，地方政府应根据当地疫情防控情况安排学校推迟开学时间。

现在中国的一些学校已经开始采用在线授课，因为为了最大限度减少人与人之间的接触，很多学生必须待在家里。

新型冠状病毒疫情暴发后，在线教育股票和数字医疗股票继上周大幅上涨之后，还在继续上涨。

一些分析师认为，自我隔离期这段时间以后可能会成为一个分水岭，标志着在线服务新时代的开启——股票行情也与之密切相关。

香港上市公司，包括与网络游戏、数字医疗服务、远程办公和远程教育等行业相关的股票，成为上周飙升的新经济类股，因为投资者们意识到革新时刻即将到来。

审校员：乔婷

审校时间：2020.4.4

五、参考译文

大多数教师从未上过网课，这对他们来说也是一件新鲜事物。他们必须学会在镜头前自然地说话，在演讲中使用红色数码笔，并通过打字评论让学生们保持在线参与感——一直集中精神对小孩子或青少年来说并不是一件容易的事。

中国的教师们一直在使用阿里巴巴的软件钉钉来上直播课。对于很多人来说，这听起来很容易，但正如来自成都的谢老师告诉《南华早报》的那样，“对于一些年长的老师来说，学习如何上直播课并不容易。昨天，我的一位同事跟我说，她仍然不知道如何使用钉钉上直播课（即使是受过了网课培训）。”

教育部近日发表声明批评了学校规定学生必须每天打卡的做法。

教育部表示，学校不应该严格规定学生每天应该学多久，也不应该强制要求学生连续几个小时拍摄自己的学习过程。

教育部还提醒学校不要让教师过度劳累，不能强制老师录播每一节课，并且禁止幼儿园开设网课。

中国教育部表示将会审慎研究制定今年高考的具体实施方案（全国大学入学考试，一般在6月举行），稍后决定今年高考是否延期，及时评估疫情对组织考试可能产生的影响。

教育部官员称，地方政府应根据当地疫情具体情况来安排延迟开学。

为了尽量减少人与人之间的互动，许多学生不得不待在家里，因此，现在有些学校采取在线学习作为一种教学方法。

新冠肺炎疫情暴发后，在线教育和数字医疗类股票继上周大幅上涨后继续上涨。

一些分析师认为，现在大家自我隔离的这段时间可能在将来会被视为一个分水岭，它将标志着在线服务以及与其密切相关的股票的新时代已经到来了。

在香港上市的与网络游戏、数字医疗服务、远程工作和远程教育相关的公司是上周新经济股中暴涨的领域，投资者们嗅到一个变革的时刻即将到来。

第四节　汉译英翻译实务

一、原文

教育部高校学生司司长王辉表示，高考工作要把考生和涉考工作人员的生命安全和身体健康放在第一位。距离高考还有将近4个月，将密切关注疫情发展变化，及时评估疫情对组织考试可能产生的影响，审慎研究制定今年高考的具体实施方案，相关工作安排会及时向社会公布。

据教育部应对新冠肺炎疫情工作领导小组办公室主任王登峰介绍，对于来自不同地区的学生，可能要采取不同的措施，每一所学校都要按照统一的部署和要求进行消杀方面的准备，来自疫情严重地区的，和确诊病人有过接触的，包括有咳嗽发烧症状的同学，可能要进行单独的隔离，其他的同学每天要测量体温，要随时关注他们身体状况的变化，这些不一定需要隔离。

来自湖北疫区的同学，在返校之前要按照湖北武汉当地实际的要求，湖北籍的学生要到外地上学首先要符合湖北当地的要求。等他们从湖北回到各自学校之后，也要进行单独的隔离。其他地方到武汉去上学的同学也是同样，在武汉地区还没有解除人员流动管控时，也不能够过去。

为了帮助偏远贫困地区的学生拓宽学习渠道，提供学习的资源支持与服务，从2月17日开始，就是下周一开始，中国教育电视台第四频道将通过直播卫星平台向全国用户传授有关课程学习资源，将覆盖偏远贫困农村地区，特别是网络信号比较弱和有线电视没有通达的地区，解决这些地区学生的学习问题。同时要指出，教育电视台播出时间是有限的，这些学习资源以小学课程资源为主，同时兼顾了初中和高中学生的学习。

此外，他还强调，有一点必须要说明，对于上新课的，要坚决防止以居家学习来完全代替学校正常的课堂教学工作，所以各地各校要认真做好开学后的教学与现在居家学习的紧密衔接。

二、学生译文初稿

Wang Hui, director of the College Students Department of the Ministry of Education, expressed that in the work of college entrance examination, top priority should be put to the life safety and health of both the students taking the exam and the staff involved in the exam. With the college entrance examination about four months away, close attention will be paid to the development of the pandemic to timely evaluate the impacts that the epidemic may have on the examination and prudently study and formulate the detailed plans for the implementation of the college entrance examination this year. The relevant work arrangement shall be released to the public in due course.

According to Wang Dengfeng, office director of the leading task force responding to the novel coronavirus in the Ministry of Education, different measures may be adopted for students from different areas, and every school has to carry out disinfection following the unified arrangement and requirement. Students from coronavirus hotspots, or students having contact history with patients diagnosed with coronavirus, as well as those showing symptoms such as coughing and fever, may need to be isolated separately. Other students do not necessarily have to be quarantined, but need to have their body temperature tested on a daily basis, and constant attention must be paid to the changes in their physical conditions.

With regards to students from Hubei which is hit hard by the epidemic, according to the local requirement in Wuhan, Hubei, they have to meet the local requirement first before returning to schools in other provinces. Upon their return to their schools from Hubei, they also need to be quarantined separately. It's the same for the students from other provinces going to study in Wuhan, and they can not travel to Wuhan either before the flow of personnel is deregulated in Wuhan area.

In order to help the students from remote and impoverished areas to broaden their learning channels and provide them with the resources and services needed in learning, starting from 27th Feb (next Monday), China Education Television Channel 4 will deliver relevant curriculum learning resources to the users across the nation through direct broadcast satellite platform, covering the remote and impoverished rural areas especially the areas with relatively weak network signal and no cable television, to resolve the learning problem for students from these areas. Meanwhile, it needs to be noted that, as the time for the broadcast on the Education Television is limited, these learning resources will be focused on the resources for the curriculum of primary schools, while also making arrangements for the learning of middle school and high school students.

In addition, he also emphasized that, another point that needs to be made clear is that, when it comes to teaching new courses, the practice of completely replacing the usual classroom teaching at school with studying from home has to be strictly prevented. Therefore, schools in every area has to be well prepared for the smooth transition from studying at home to teaching at school after school reopens.

——译员：牛婷

三、学生译文修改稿

Wang Hui, director of the College Students Department of the Ministry of Education, expressed that in the work of gaokao, top priority should be put to the life safety and health of both the students taking the exam and the staff involved in the exam. With the college entrance examination about four months away, close attention will be paid to the development of the coronavirus epidemic situation to timely evaluate the impacts that the epidemic may have on the examination and prudently study and formulate the detailed plans for the implementation of the college entrance examination this year. The relevant work arrangement shall be announced to the public in due course.

According to Wang Dengfeng, office director of the leading task force responding to the novel coronavirus in the Ministry of Education, different measures may be adopted for students from different areas, and every school has to carry out disinfection following the unified arrangement and requirement. Students coming from areas hit hard by the epidemic, and those with close contacts of confirmed cases, as well as those showing symptoms such as coughing and fever, may need to be quarantined separately. Other students do not necessarily have to be quarantined, but need to have their body temperature tested on a daily basis, and constant attention must be paid to the changes of their physical conditions.

With regards to students from Hubei province which is hit

设置格式[T]: 缩进: 首行缩进: 2 字符

删除[T]: colleg

删除[T]: e entrance examination

删除[T]: pandemic

删除[T]: release

删除[T]: d

删除[T]: coronavirus hotspots, or students having

删除[T]: history with patients diagnosed with coronavirus,

删除[T]: isolated

删除[T]: in

hard by the epidemic, according to the local requirement in Wuhan, Hubei, they have to meet the local requirement first before returning to schools in other provinces. Upon their return to their schools from Hubei, they also need to be quarantined separately. It's the same for the students from other provinces going to study in Wuhan, and they can not travel to Wuhan either before the flow of personnel is deregulated in Wuhan area.

In order to help the students from remote and impoverished areas with poor internet accessibility to broaden their learning channels, starting from 27th Feb (next Monday), China Education Television Channel 4 will deliver relevant curriculum learning resources to the users across the nation through direct broadcast satellite platform, covering the remote and impoverished rural areas especially the areas with relatively weak network signal and no cable television. Meanwhile, it needs to be noted that, as the time for the broadcast on the Education Television is limited, these learning resources will be focused on the resources for the curriculum of primary schools, while also making arrangements for the learning of middle school and high school students.

删除[T]: and provide them with the resources and services needed in learning,

删除[T]: , to resolve the learning problem for students from these areas.

In addition, he also emphasized that, when it comes to teaching new courses, the practice of completely replacing the usual classroom teaching at school with studying from home has to be strictly prevented. Therefore, schools in every area

删除[T]: another point that needs to be made clear is that,

has to be well prepared for the smooth transition from studying at home to teaching at school after school reopens.

审校员：乔婷

审校时间：2020.4.4

四、学生译文终稿

Wang Hui, director of the College Students Department of the Ministry of Education, expressed that in the work of gaokao, top priority should be put to the life safety and health of both the students taking the exam and the staff involved in the exam. With the college entrance examination about four months away, close attention will be paid to the development of the coronavirus epidemic situation to timely evaluate the impacts that the epidemic may have on the examination and prudently study and formulate the detailed plans for the implementation of the college entrance examination this year. The relevant work arrangement shall be announced to the public in due course.

According to Wang Dengfeng, office director of the leading task force responding to the novel coronavirus in the Ministry of Education, different measures may be adopted for students from different areas, and every school has to carry out disinfection following the unified arrangement and requirement. Students coming from areas hit hard by the epidemic, and those with close contacts of confirmed cases, as well as those showing symptoms such as coughing and fever, may need to be quarantined separately. Other students do not necessarily have to be quarantined, but need to have their body temperature tested on a daily basis, and constant attention must be paid to the changes of their physical conditions.

With regards to students from Hubei province which is hit hard by the epidemic, according to the local requirement in Wuhan, Hubei, they have to meet the local requirement first before returning to schools in other provinces. Upon their return to their schools from Hubei, they also need to be quarantined separately. It's the same for the students from other provinces going to study in Wuhan, and they can not travel to Wuhan either before the flow of personnel is deregulated in Wuhan area.

In order to help the students from remote and impoverished areas with poor internet accessibility to broaden their learning channels, starting from 27th Feb (next Monday),

China Education Television Channel 4 will deliver relevant curriculum learning resources to the users across the nation through direct broadcast satellite platform, covering the remote and impoverished rural areas especially the areas with relatively weak network signal and no cable television. Meanwhile, it needs to be noted that, as the time for the broadcast on the Education Television is limited, these learning resources will be focused on the resources for the curriculum of primary schools, while also making arrangements for the learning of middle school and high school students.

In addition, he also emphasized that, when it comes to teaching new courses, the practice of completely replacing the usual classroom teaching at school with studying from home has to be strictly prevented. Therefore, schools in every area has to be well prepared for the smooth transition from studying at home to teaching at school after school reopens.

审校员：乔婷

审校时间：2020.4.4

五、参考译文

"Top priority should be put to the life safety and health of both the students taking the exam and the staff involved in the exam. With the college entrance examination about four months away, the Ministry of Education（MOE）will pay close attention to the development of the coronavirus epidemic situation, and promptly assess the conditions that might affect gaokao together with the relevant departments.The relevant work arrangement will be announced to the public in a timely manner" ,said Wang Hui, director of the ministry's Department of College Students Affairs.

According to Wang Dengfeng, office director of the leading task force responding to the novel coronavirus in the Ministry of Education, different measures may be adopted for students from different areas, and every school has to carry out disinfection following the unified arrangement and requirement. Students coming from areas hit hard by the epidemic, and those with close contracts of confirmed cases or those having symptoms such as fever or cough, might need to be put under quarantine. Other students do not necessarily have to be quarantined, but need to have their body temperature tested on a daily basis, and constant attention must be paid to the changes in their physical conditions.

With regards to students from Hubei which is hit hard by the epidemic, Students from Hubei province, where the epicenter city of Wuhan is located, will not be able to leave for schools outside the province until they meet local requirement, and they should be quarantined when they return to their schools, he said. It's the same for the students from other provinces going to study in Wuhan, and they can not travel to Wuhan either before the flow of personnel is deregulated in Wuhan area.

For students in remote or rural areas with poor internet accessibility to broaden their learning channels, a television channel by China Education Television will start airing classes on Monday(27th Feb.) so they can study at home. China Education Television Channel 4 will deliver relevant curriculum learning resources to the users across the nation through direct broadcast satellite platform, covering the remote and impoverished rural areas especially the areas with relatively weak network signal and no cable television. Meanwhile, it needs to be noted that, as the time for the broadcast on the Education Television is limited, these learning resources will be focused on the resources for the curriculum of primary schools, while also making arrangements for the learning of middle school and high school students.

"Online courses are only temporary measures taken during the epidemic, so when the new semester begins, schools should not replace classroom teaching with online classes, schools in every area has to be well prepared for the smooth transition from studying at home to teaching at school after school reopens." he added.

第五节 翻译实务评析

一、词法分析

在教育类文本的翻译中，一词多义现象较为常见。例如，在原文（英译汉）中，"released"一词有"释放、发泄、免除、公开、发表"等多种含义，译者需要根据具体语境灵活选用恰当的词义，最终选定"发表"这一词义。此外，词性转换也尤为常见。例如，在原文（汉译英）中，"密切关注疫情发展变化"一句中，"密切关注"为动词，体现了汉语的动态性。译者贴合英语表达习惯，选择形容词搭配名词的形式，将其译为"close attention"，体现了英语的静态性。

二、句法分析

例如，在原文（英译汉）中，首段第二句中，"have to"后并列了三个动词引导的三个并列的分句，对翻译造成了一定的困难，译者采用直译法，但在翻译过程中，使用破折号等连接方式，让译文符合译入语读者的阅读习惯。教育文本中涉及有关教育政策、方针等专有名词，是已经发生的状态，因此翻译时应注意时态的选择。在原文（英译汉）“released”“warned”等词都用了过去时。从语态来看，汉语多主动，英语多被动。译者应当注意这两种语态的转换。例如，在原文（汉译英）中，首段“高考工作要把考生和涉考工作人员的生命安全和身体健康放在第一位”一句为主动形式，但蕴含被动语态，“考试和涉考工作人员的生命安全和身体健康”应当是“被放在高考工作中的第一位”，因此译者将其译为“top priority should be put to...”，符合英语多被动语态的特征。

三、语篇分析

教育文本结构严谨、逻辑清晰、层次分明，语篇内部衔接系统完整。因此，译者在翻译过程中应注重原文的衔接与连贯等特征。在教育文本中，多用代词替代上文中已经出现过的内容。例如，在原文（英译汉）第五段及第六段中，均使用代词“it”来替代第三段中提及的“The Ministry of Education”，而译者在翻译时将代词指明要点，均译为“教育部”，能够明确表达原文信息。英语中多用介词增强语篇的衔接性。例如，在原文（汉译英）中，“距离高考还有将近4个月”一句本身没有衔接词，而译者在翻译时使用“with”这一介词来增进译文的衔接，有利于目的语读者对原文信息的接受与理解。

【课外拓展】

你校与国外知名大学共同举办线上教育论坛，请你和团队分角色扮演，完成模拟口译情境。

文献参考

[1]车明明．应用翻译理论创新与翻译教育：思考与对策——第六届全国应用翻译研讨会综述[J]，中国翻译，2015(04)：95-97．

[2]付非宇．教育类著作Digital Personalization in Early Childhood(Chapter5-6)英汉翻译实践报告[D]．哈尔滨：黑龙江大学，2019．

[3]方梦之．我国的应用翻译：定位与学术研究——2003全国应用翻译研讨会侧记[J]．中国翻译，2003(06)：49-51．

[4]韩子满．应用翻译：实践与理论研究[J]．中国科技翻译，2005(04)：50-53+63．

[5]黄忠廉．翻译项目管理[M]．北京:国防工业出版社,2014．

[6]雷琼雅．教育类论文英汉翻译实践报告[D],武汉:华中师范大学,2017．

[7]王雪宁．教育类研究报告 Measuring and Assessing Internationalization 英汉翻译实践报告[D]．哈尔滨:黑龙江大学,2019．

[8]杨盼．功能翻译理论视角下教育文本翻译浅析[J]．锦州医科大学学报(社会科学版),2018(04):130-132+140．

[9]张静．关于应用文体翻译的实践报告[D]．青岛:青岛科技大学,2013．

[10]周险峰．教育文本理解论[D]．上海:华东师范大学,2006．

第六章　科技翻译

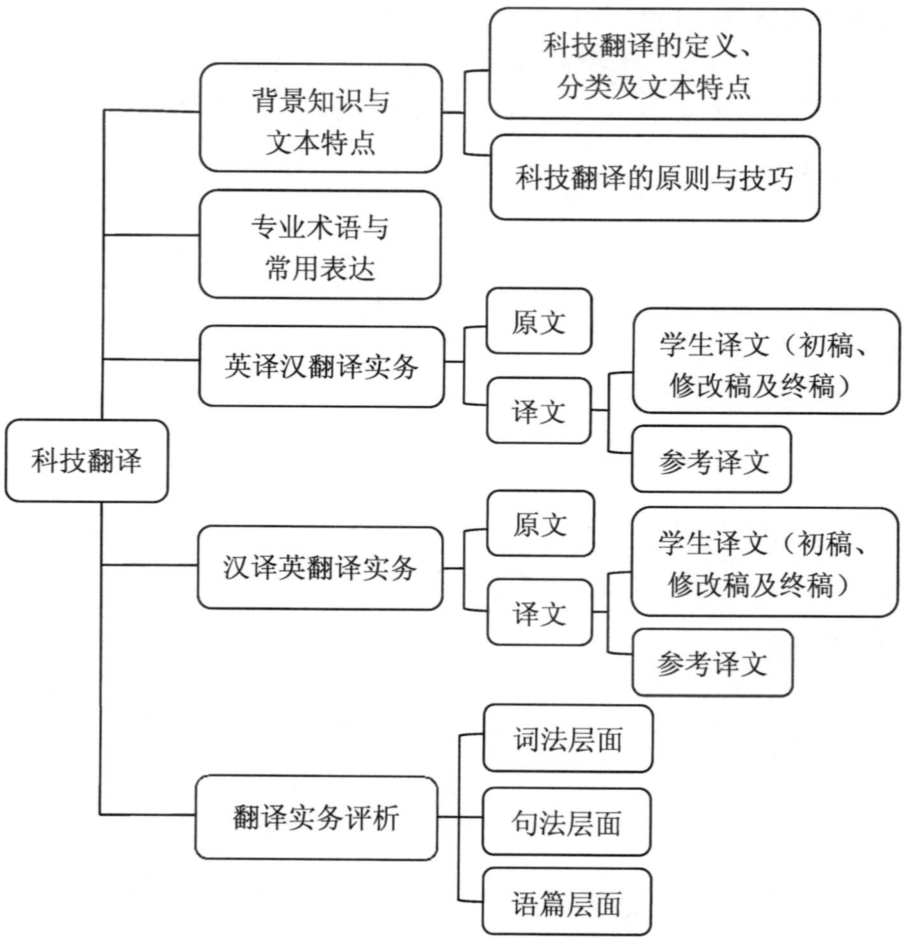
科技翻译
背景知识与文本特点
科技翻译的定义、分类及文本特点
科技翻译的原则与技巧
专业术语与常用表达
英译汉翻译实务
原文
译文
学生译文（初稿、修改稿及终稿）
参考译文
汉译英翻译实务
原文
译文
学生译文（初稿、修改稿及终稿）
参考译文
翻译实务评析
词法层面
句法层面
语篇层面

第一节　背景知识与文本特点

一、科技翻译定义、分类及文本特点

科技翻译是指将自然科学和工程技术方面的著作、论文、研究报告、技术标准、科技产品指南、科技图书和学术讲演中所使用的语言翻译成另一种语言。科技文本主要包括专业科技文本和普通科技文本，前者主要指某一科研领域内具有较高学术水平的专著、科研论文、实验报告等，其读者群体主要为科学家、大学教授、高级科研工作者、行业专家等专业人士，后者主要指一些普及科技知识的读物、说明书、操作指南、安全手册等，读者群体主要是学生、客户、工人等非专业的普通读者。此类文本具有清晰准确、精炼严密、专业规范等特点，同时科普类文章也具备知识性和趣味性相结合的特点，其语言较为生动活泼，甚至包含一定的文学色彩。

二、科技翻译的原则与技巧

因不同文体、不同领域的翻译各有其特点，科技翻译不能完全照搬其它文本的译法，为使译文忠实于原文，需注意以下几个原则：语义准确，表达通顺，措辞贴切。科技翻译注重语篇逻辑性、思维的严密性和表达的准确性，多使用专业术语和缩略语，因此在翻译过程中要高度把握准确性原则。科技翻译的社会价值在于为专业技术人员、学者等提供准确资料和信息，若逐词死译，语句不通，势必会造成译文生涩难懂。在保证译文准确忠实，通顺规范的基础上，还要追求措辞贴切优美。科技文献虽注重客观性，但如果译文可以恰如其分地使用修辞、形容、比喻等手法，必然会使科技知识充满乐趣。基于科技文本自身的词汇、语法及句法特点，译者在翻译过程中要注重生僻短语的翻译，掌握长句运用以及学习相关知识。总的来说，专业科技文本的翻译要表述准确，避免歧义；叙述清楚，富有逻辑；注重信息传递，用语专业、规范，可适当使用解释性语言。而科普类科技文本除了要表意清楚，语篇富有逻辑，注重信息传递外，还要兼顾语言形式，适当保留原文修辞手段和语言风格，使译文兼具科学性、知识性和趣味性，既能满足读者的知识需求，又能满足他们的审美需求。

第二节　专业术语与常用表达

ST	TT
1.反转录病毒	retrovirus
2.表达筛选	expression screening
3.质粒载体	plasmid vector
4.前病毒	provirus
5.表型	phenotype
6.转导	transduction
7.功能检测	functional assay
8.识别基因	reporter gene
9.亲异的	xenotropic
10.黏附分子	adhesion molecule
11.突变分子	mutant molecule
12.转录因子	transcription factor
13.大肠杆菌	escherichia coli
14.线粒体	mitochondria
15.荧光定位	fluorescence localization
16.亚细胞的	subcellular
17.苜蓿	alfalfa
18.评论	critique
19.取消对.....的管制	deregulate
20.经验主义的,完全根据经验的	empirical
21.花粉	pollen
22.授花粉器	pollinator
23.菜籽油	canola
24.不合理的	unconscionable

续表

ST	TT
25.杀虫剂	pesticide
26.连锁反应	ripple effect
27.草料	forage
28.除草剂	herbicide
29.毒素	toxin
30.枯萎病	blight
31.饥荒	famine
32.危害	compromise
33.杂合子	heterozygote
34.移码突变	frameshift mutation
35.阅读框	reading frame
36.原噬菌体	prophage
37.液相杂交	liquid hybridization
38.叶绿体基因组	chloroplast genome
39.野生型等位基因	wild-type allele
40.诱导型启动子	inducible promoter
41.烟草花叶病毒	tobacco mosaic virus
42.延伸因子	elongation factor
43.严紧型质粒	stringent plasmid
44.性染色体	sex chromosome
45.正向突变	forward mutation
46.转录间隔区	transcribed spacer
47.增强子	enhancer
48.异核体	heterokaryon/ heterocaryon
49.异构酶	isomerase
50.杂交瘤	hybridoma

第三节　英译汉翻译实务

一、原文

Resulting contamination of non-GE and organic alfalfa hay and seed would devastate livelihoods and organic industry.

The National Organic Coalition（NOC） today announced that more than 200,000 people submitted comments to the United States Department of Agriculture （USDA） critiquing the substance and conclusions of its Draft Environmental Impact Statement （DEIS） on Genetically Engineered （GE） Alfalfa. Groups, including NOC, Center for Food Safety （CFS), Organic Consumers Association, Food & Water Watch, CREDO Action and Food Democracy Now, mobilized their communities to help generate the unprecedented number of comments.

In addition, more than 300 public interest organizations, farmers, dairies, retailers and organic food producers from the U.S. and Canada delivered a strongly worded letter to USDA, calling upon it to deny approval of Monsanto's genetically engineered, Roundup Ready alfalfa （GE alfalfa). The letter cites the inevitable contamination of organic and non-GE alfalfa hay and seeds and threats to the viability of organic dairies, livestock, and meat and dairy producers as reasons for urging the denial. NOC, Organic Valley, Whole Foods, National Cooperative Grocers Association, CFS and others agree that it would be irresponsible government policy to approve GE alfalfa in the absence of legal requirements holding companies accountable for GE contamination, as is currently the case.

In 2006, CFS sued USDA for its illegal approval of Monsanto's GE alfalfa. USDA failed to conduct an environmental impact statement （EIS), as required by law, before deregulating the crop. The federal courts sided with CFS and banned GE alfalfa plantings until USDA analyzed the impacts of GE alfalfa on the environment, farmers and the public. Today marks the deadline for submitting public comments on the draft EIS, which recommends approving Monsanto's GE alfalfa.

USDA's EIS claims that organic consumers do not care about GE contamination of their food, despite overwhelming evidence to the contrary. Consumer surveys show that 75 percent or more of respondents repeatedly say that they do not want to eat GE contaminated food and cite their desire to avoid GE food as one of the top five reasons for buying organic.

二、学生译文初稿

造成非转基因和有机苜蓿干草和种子的污染将破坏生计和有机产业。

美国国家有机联盟（NOC）今天宣布，超过20万人向美国农业部（USDA）提交了评论，批评了其关于基因工程苜蓿的环境影响声明（DEIS）草案的实质和结论。包括美国国家有机联盟（NOC），食品安全中心（CFS），有机消费者协会，食品和水源监督机构以及食品民主现在在内的团体动员了他们的社区，以帮助他们产生前所未有的评论数量。

此外，美国和加拿大的300多个公共利益组织，农民，乳制品，零售商和有机食品生产商向美国农业部发表了措辞严谨的信，呼吁美国农业部拒绝批准孟山都公司的基因工程农达苜蓿（基因苜蓿）。该信援引了有机和非转基因苜蓿干草和种子不可避免的污染，并威胁有机乳制品，牲畜以及肉类和奶制品生产商的生存，这是敦促拒绝的理由。美国国家有机联盟，有机谷，全食，国家合作食品杂货商协会，食品安全中心等同意，在没有法律要求（要求公司对基因污染负责）的情况下批准基因苜蓿是不负责任的政府政策。

2006年，食品安全中心起诉美国农业部非法批准孟山都基因苜蓿。美国农业部未能按照法律要求执行环境影响声明（EIS），然后才对农作物放松管制。联邦法院支持CFS并禁止种植基因苜蓿，直到美国农业部分析基因苜蓿对环境，农民和公众的影响。今天是对EIS草案提交公众意见的截止日期，该草案建议批准孟山都的基因苜蓿。

美国农业部的EIS声称，尽管有大量相反的证据，有机消费者也不关心基因对食物的污染。消费者调查显示，有75%或更多的受访者反复表示，他们不想吃被基因污染的食物，并希望避免食用基因食物，这是购买有机食品的五大理由之一。

——译员：张胜霞

三、学生译文修改稿

造成非转基因和有机苜蓿干草和种子的污染将破坏生计和有机产业。

今天，美国国家有机联盟（NOC）宣布，超过 20 万人向美国农业部（USDA）提交了针对基因工程苜蓿提出的关于“环境影响声明草案（DEIS）”的影响和实质的评论意见。现在，包括美国国家有机联盟（NOC），食品安全中心（CFS），有机消费者协会，食品和水源监督机构以及食品民主等机构在内社会团体动员其成员参与到这次前所未有评论行动中来。

此外，美国和加拿大的 300 多个公共利益组织，农民，乳制品，零售商和有机食品生产商向美国农业部投递了措辞严谨的信函，呼吁美国农业部拒绝批准孟山都公司的基因工程农达苜蓿（基因苜蓿）。信中指出有机和非转基因苜蓿干草和种子有不可避免的污染，并且它威胁到有机乳制品，牲畜以及肉类和奶制品生产商的生存，这就是大家拒绝的缘由。美国国家有机联盟，有机谷，全食，国家合作食品杂货商协会，食品安全中心等机构都认为，在没有法律要求（要求公司对基因污染负责）的情况下，批准 GE 苜蓿是不负责任的政府政策。

2006 年，食品安全中心起诉美国农业部非法批准孟山都基因苜蓿。美国农业部未能按照法律要求执行环境影响声明（EIS），然后才对农作物放松管制。联邦法院支持食品安全中心并禁止种植基因苜蓿，直到美国农业部分析苜蓿对环境，农民和公众的影响。今天是对 EIS 草案提交公众意见的截止日期，该草案建议批准孟山都的基因苜蓿。

删除[马]：今天

删除[马]：评论，批评了其关于

删除[马]：（DEIS）

删除[马]：结论

删除[马]：NOC

删除[马]：观察，CREDO 行动和

删除[马]：现在在内的团体动员了他们的社区，以帮助他们产生前所未有的评论数量。

删除[马]：发表

删除[马]：信

删除[马]：该

删除[马]：信援引了

删除[马]：是

删除[马]：敦促

删除[马]：理由

删除[马]：NOC

删除[马]：CFS

删除[马]：同意

删除[马]：CFS

删除[马]：GE

美国农业部的EIS声称，有机食品消费者也不关心基因对食物的污染，尽管大量的事实与此相反。消费者调查显示，有75%或更多的受访者反复强调，他们不想吃被基因污染的食物，并希望避免食用基因食品，这是购买有机食品的五大理由之一。

删除[马]：尽管有大量相反的证据，

删除[马]：表示

审校员：马晓娟

审校时间：2020.6.15

四、学生译文终稿

造成非转基因和有机苜蓿干草和种子的污染将破坏生计和有机产业。

今天，美国国家有机联盟（NOC）宣布，超过20万人向美国农业部（USDA）提交了针对基因工程苜蓿提出的关于“环境影响声明草案（DEIS）”的影响和实质的评论意见。现在，包括美国国家有机联盟（NOC），食品安全中心（CFS），有机消费者协会，食品和水源监督机构以及食品民主等机构在内社会团体动员其成员参与到这次前所未有评论行动中来。

此外，美国和加拿大的300多个公共利益组织，农民，乳制品，零售商和有机食品生产商向美国农业部投递了措辞严谨的信函，呼吁美国农业部拒绝批准孟山都公司的基因工程农达苜蓿（基因苜蓿）。信中指出有机和非转基因苜蓿干草和种子有不可避免的污染，并且它威胁到有机乳制品，牲畜以及肉类和奶制品生产商的生存，这就是大家拒绝的缘由。美国国家有机联盟，有机谷，全食，国家合作食品杂货商协会，食品安全中心等机构都认为，在没有法律要求（要求公司对基因污染负责）的情况下，批准GE苜蓿是不负责任的政府政策。

2006年，食品安全中心起诉美国农业部非法批准孟山都基因苜蓿。美国农业部未能按照法律要求执行环境影响声明（EIS），然后才对农作物放松管制。联邦法院支持食品安全中心并禁止种植基因苜蓿，直到美国农业部分析苜蓿对环境，农民和公众的影响。今天是对EIS草案提交公众意见的截止日期，该草案建议批准孟山都的基因苜蓿。

美国农业部的EIS声称，有机食品消费者也不关心基因对食物的污染，尽管大量的事实与此相反。消费者调查显示，有75%或更多的受访者反复强调，他们不想吃被基因污染的食物，并希望避免食用基因食品，这是购买有机食品的五大理由之一。

审校员：马晓娟

审校时间：2020.6.15

五、参考译文

基因工程有机苜蓿干草和种子造成的污染会危及生计和有机产业。今天，全国有机联盟(NOC)宣布，超过20万人向美国农业部(USDA)提出反对该机构“环境影响报告书草案(DEIS)”中对转基因苜蓿的评论意见。现在，包括全国有机联盟、食品安全中心(CFS)、有机消费者协会、食品和水源监督机构以及食品民主等机构在内的社会团体均动员他们的成员发表评论来促成这一前所未有的为数众多的行动。

此外，300多个公益组织、农民、奶制品供应商、零售商和来自美国及加拿大的有机食品生产商向美国农业部发表了措辞强烈的信函，呼吁它拒绝批准孟山都公司的基因工程草甘膦苜蓿(基因苜蓿)。信中列举了该基因工程对有机非基因工程苜蓿干草及种子不可避免的污染，以及对有机乳制品、牲畜、肉类和乳制品生产商生存发展的威胁作为要求拒绝的原因。全国有机联盟、有机谷、全食、全国杂货商联合协会、食品安全中心和其他团体都认为，如果像现在这样在没有法律要求公司要对基因工程造成的污染负责的情况下批准基因工程苜蓿，那将是不负责任的政府才会有的政策。

2006年，食品安全中心起诉美国农业部非法批准了孟山都公司的基因苜蓿。美国农业部没有按照法律要求在解除对这种作物的管控之前执行环境影响报告书(EIS)。联邦法院站在食品安全中心一边，禁止基因苜蓿的种植直到美国农业部分析完成基因苜蓿对环境、农民和公众的影响。今天是对环境影响报告书草案提交公众评论的最后期限，这个草案赞成孟山都公司的基因苜蓿。

美国农业部的环境影响报告书称有机食品的消费者不用担心基因工程会对他们的食物造成污染，尽管大量的事实与此相反。消费者调查显示，75%以上的调查对象反复地说他们不愿意吃被基因工程污染的食物，他们购买有机食品的五个原因之中最重要的一条就是想要避免购买基因工程生产的食物。

第四节　汉译英翻译实务

一、原文

逆转录病毒介导的表达克隆在20世纪90年代中期发展起来。借助逆转录病毒载体的cDNA基因库建设和用质粒载体没有区别。根据这个方法可以生成单向或双向的cDNA文库。互补的DNA用oligo-dT或随机六聚体核苷酸作引物来生产。文库以DNA溶液的形式保存，并且使用包装细胞系转换成逆转录病毒。要生成代表并包含cDNA文库的高复杂性的逆转录病毒，建议使用293包装细胞系，瞬时包装效率会更高。病毒的遗传特性包括高效价的逆转录病毒用来感染靶细胞，被感染的细胞可具有特定的性状而被选择出来。然后完整的cDNA可以用聚合酶链式反应（PCR）或逆转录PCR来恢复，来确定哪些cDNA与表现型有关哪些与基因序列有关。

逆转录病毒介导的表达克隆的方法是有效的，因为在每个细胞的前病毒整合的数量是有限的。因此，它没有必要像在COS7细胞的常规方法一样恢复和重新引入质粒。逆转录病毒介导的表达克隆，感染效率应控制在10%和30%之间，以尽可能避免多个整合到一个细胞内。另外，我们可以通过转染一个辅助子构建包含gag-pol和env基因到一个独立的克隆来回收整合的逆转录病毒，在cDNA文库转导后已经获得了特定表型。在这种情况下，回收的逆转录病毒感染靶细胞从而确定其中哪个整合是与表现型有关的。

二、学生译文初稿

Retrovirus-mediated expression cloning was developed in the mid-1990s. There is no difference in the construction of cDNA gene pool by retrovirus vector and plasmid vector. According to this method, unidirectional or bidirectional cDNA libraries can be generated. Complementary DNA is produced using oligo-dT primers or random hexamer nucleotides primers. Libraries are stored as DNA solutions and converted into retroviruses using packaged cell lines. To generate a highly complex retrovirus that represents and contains a cDNA library, it is recommended to use 293 to package cell lines. Instantaneous packaging is more efficient. The genetic characteristics of the virus include the use of highly efficient retroviruses to infect target cells, which can be selected for specific traits. The complete cDNA can then be restored by polymerase chain reaction（PCR） or reverse transcription PCR to determine which cDNA is related to phenotype and which is related to gene sequence.

The method of Retroviral-mediated expression cloning is effective because the number of provirus integrations is limited in per cell. Therefore, it is not necessary to restore and regenerate the introduced plasmid, which is like the conventional method in COS7 cells. For retrovirus-mediated expression cloning, the infection efficiency should be controlled between 10% and 30% to avoid as many integrations into one cell as possible. In addition, we can recover an integrated retrovirus by transfecting a helper to construct containing the protein and envelope protein genes into a separate clone which has acquired a specific phenotype after transduction of the cDNA library. In this case, the recovered retroviruses infect the target cells to determine which of these integrations is phenotypically related.

——译员：王婷婷

三、学生译文修改稿

Retrovirus-mediated expression cloning was developed in the mid-1990s. The construction of cDNA gene pool in a retrovirus vector is not different from that in a plasmid vector. According to this method, unidirectional or bidirectional cDNA libraries can be generated. Complementary DNA is produced using oligo-dT primers or random hexamer nucleotides primers. Libraries are stored as DNA solutions and converted into retroviruses using packaged cell lines. To generate a highly complex retrovirus that represents and contains a cDNA library, it is recommended to use 293 to package cell lines. Instantaneous packaging is more efficient. The genetic characteristics of the virus include the use of highly efficient retroviruses to infect target cells, which can be selected for specific traits. The complete cDNA can then be restored by polymerase chain reaction (PCR) or reverse transcription PCR

删除[马]: There is no difference in t

删除[马]: by

删除[马]: and

to determine which cDNA is related to phenotype and which is related to gene sequence.

The method of retroviral-mediated expression cloning is efficient because the number of provirus integrations is limited in per cell. Therefore, it is not necessary to restore and regenerate the introduced plasmid, which is like the conventional method in COS7 cells. For retrovirus-mediated expression cloning, the infection efficiency should be controlled between 10% and 30% to avoid as many integrations into one cell as possible. In addition, we can recover an integrated retrovirus by transfecting a helper to construct containing the protein and envelope protein genes into a separate clone which has acquired a specific phenotype after transduction of the cDNA library. In this case, the recovered retroviruses infect the target cells to determine which of these integrations is phenotypically related.

删除[马]: R

审校员：马晓娟

审校时间：2020.6.15

四、学生译文终稿

Retrovirus-mediated expression cloning was developed in the mid-1990s. The construction of cDNA gene pool in a retrovirus vector is not different from that in a plasmid vector. According to this method, unidirectional or bidirectional cDNA libraries can be generated. Complementary DNA is produced using oligo-dT primers or random hexamer nucleotides primers. Libraries are stored as DNA solutions and converted into retroviruses using packaged cell lines. To generate a highly complex retrovirus that represents and contains a cDNA library, it is recommended to use 293 to package cell lines. Instantaneous packaging is more efficient. The genetic characteristics of the virus include the use of highly efficient retroviruses to infect target cells, which can be selected for specific traits. The complete cDNA can then be restored by polymerase chain reaction (PCR) or reverse transcription PCR to determine which cDNA is related to phenotype and which is related to gene sequence.

The method of retroviral-mediated expression cloning is efficient because the number of provirus integrations is limited in per cell. Therefore, it is not necessary to restore and regenerate the introduced plasmid, which is like the conventional method in COS7 cells. For retrovirus-mediated expression cloning, the infection efficiency should be controlled between 10% and 30% to avoid as many integrations into one cell as possible. In addition, we can recover an integrated retrovirus by transfecting a helper to construct containing the protein and envelope protein genes into a separate clone which has acquired a specific phenotype after transduction of the cDNA library. In this case, the recovered retroviruses infect the target cells to determine which of these integrations is phenotypically related.

审校员：马晓娟

审校时间：2020.6.15

五、参考译文

Retrovirus-mediated expression cloning was developed in the mid-1990s. Construction of a cDNA library in a retrovirus vector is not different from that in a plasmid vector. One can generate either unidirectional or bi-directional cDNA libraries depending on the intended application. Complementary DNAs are generated using either oligo-dT primers or random hexamer nucleotide primers. The library is kept as DNA solution, and is converted to retroviruses by using packaging cell lines. To generate retroviruses that represent and cover a high complexity of cDNA libraries, it is recommended to use 293-based packaging cell lines that are efficient in transient packaging. The genetic character of the viruses containing high-titer retroviruses is used to infect target cells, and the infected cells are selected for the phenotype of interest. The integrated cDNA then is recovered by genomic polymerase chain reaction(PCR)or reverse transcriptase (RT)-PCR to determine which cDNA is responsible for the phenotype and which cDNA is subjected to the sequence.

The method of retrovirus-mediated expression cloning is efficient because the number of the provirus integrations in each cell is limited. Therefore, it is not necessary to recover and reintroduce the plasmid from and into the cells repeatedly as in the conventional method using COS7 cells. In retrovirus-mediated expression cloing, the infection efficiency should be controlled between 10% and 30% to avoid multiple integration in a cell as much as possible. Alternatively, one can recover the integrated retroviruses by transfecting a helper construct harboring gag-pol and env genes into the isolated clone that has acquired a phenotype of interest after transduction of the cDNA library. In this case, the recovered retroviruses are infected with the target cells to determine which integration was responsible for the phenotype.

第五节　翻译实务评析

一、词法分析

科技翻译文本专业性强且专有词汇较多，其语言具备客观和正式的特点。科技文本属于信息型文本，在翻译中多采取直译的翻译方法，力求准确传达出原文的内容。对于专业术语的翻译，首先需要明白其含义，再通过官方渠道进行查询，看有无固定翻译，如“United States Department of Agriculture（USDA)”的官方翻译为“美国农业部”，可直接采用，以保证专业术语翻译的准确性。

二、句法分析

英语长难句中可能包含多个从句，从句与从句之间的关系有并列、包含与被包含、镶嵌等。因此，译者在翻译前应对长难句进行分析，弄清楚从句之间的关系。由于英语是形合语言，词语或分句之间用语言形式手段连接起来表达语法和逻辑关系；中文是意合语言，词语与分句之间不能用语言形式手段连接。其中的语法意义和逻辑关系通过词语或分句的含义表达，且英语多长句，汉语多短句，因此在翻译时应仔细分析句子成分，并根据目的语语言特征与表达习惯，将句子做动态化处理。

三、语篇分析

本章所选翻译练习讲述逆转录病毒介导的表达筛选、基本原理和应用，文章结构层次清晰，主题明确。科技文本的语言相对正式、客观，所以在翻译时，尽可能避免口语化，以保留原文语言风格。此外，文本内容专业性强，专业词汇偏多，在翻译中主要采取直译的翻译方法，力求准确传达出原文信息。

【课外拓展】

请结合计算机辅助翻译的相关知识，进行语料库练习，并录屏。

文献参考

[1]甘成英．英文工程文献的翻译原则与处理方法[J]．外国语言文学研究，2008(2):1-5.

[2]高华丽．中外翻译简史[M]．杭州:浙江大学出版社,2009.

[3]黄忠廉．翻译项目管理[M]．北京:国防工业出版社,2014.

[4]陶全胜．科技翻译教程[M]．北京:清华大学出版社,2019.

[5]王海燕．英汉语篇翻译中替代手段的转换[J]．吉林省教育学院学报(学科版),2011(1):46-47.

[6]郑国锋．英汉替代形式对比及翻译中的几点思考[J]．华东理工大学学报(社会科学版),2006(1):108-113.

[7]周光文．科技英语翻译与写作[M]．北京:科学出版社,2015.

[8]张惠展,贾林芝．基因工程[M]．2版．北京:高等教育出版社,2010.

第七章　新闻翻译

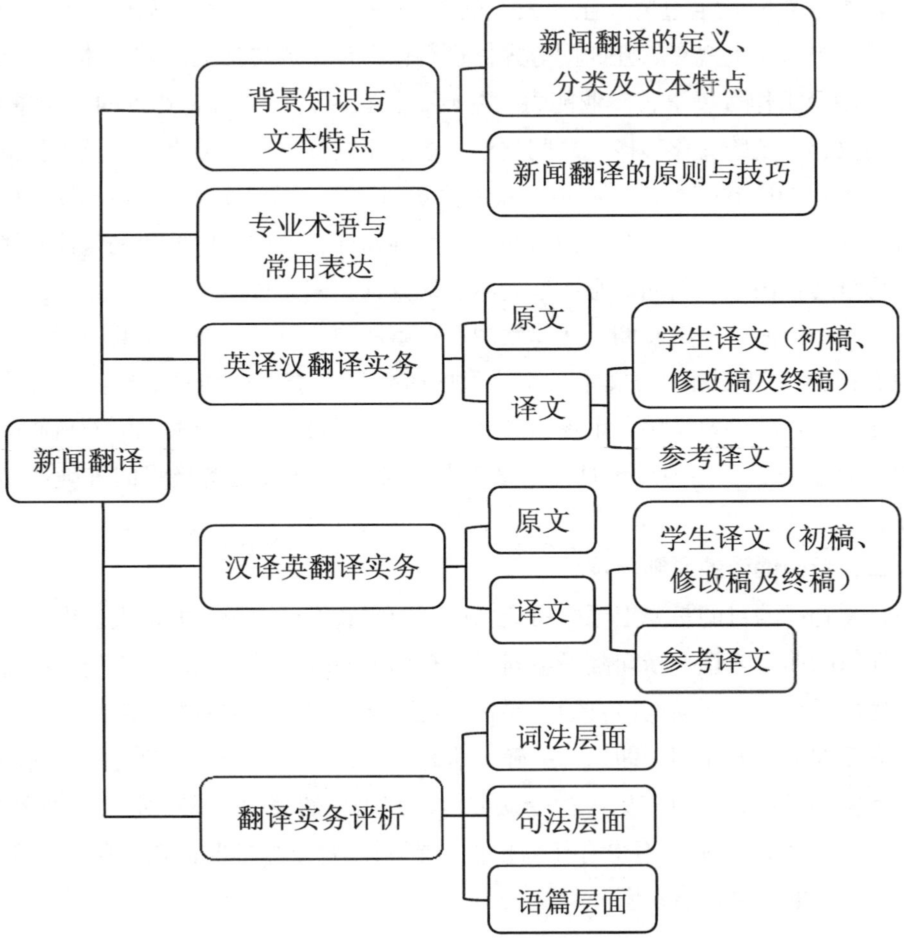
新闻翻译
背景知识与文本特点
新闻翻译的定义、分类及文本特点
新闻翻译的原则与技巧
专业术语与常用表达
英译汉翻译实务
原文
译文
学生译文（初稿、修改稿及终稿）
参考译文
汉译英翻译实务
原文
译文
学生译文（初稿、修改稿及终稿）
参考译文
翻译实务评析
词法层面
句法层面
语篇层面

第一节　背景知识与文本特点

一、新闻翻译定义、分类及文本特点

新闻是对刚发生过的、正在发生的或过去发生却是近期才发现的有价值事件，通过报纸、电视台、互联网等媒体进行信息记录或传播的一种文体。新闻翻译是指翻译工作者以语言专业能力为基础，根据不同语言文化背景和文化意识，对新闻内容实现跨文化转换。新闻类型可按照不同标准进行分类。按照事件的性质可分为："硬新闻"（hard news）和"软新闻"（soft news）；按照事实发生的状态可分为：突发性新闻、持续性新闻、周期性新闻；按照新闻发生的地区与影响范围可分为：国际性新闻、全国性新闻、地方性新闻；按照反映社会生活内容可分为：政治新闻、经济新闻、法律新闻、军事新闻、科技新闻、文娱新闻、体育新闻、社会新闻。新闻类文本具有明显的时效性、准确性和政治性。在现代社会，随着科技的迅速发展和市场的激烈竞争，人们对新闻格外关注。而新闻翻译作为强有力的表达国内外事件的重要工具，需要其译文具备极强的准确性和规范性。

二、新闻翻译的原则与技巧

新闻翻译的目的是要把原语的意思尽可能准确无误地用目的语表达出来，不能有任何的曲解之意。新闻翻译不同于其它翻译的一个重要原因在于新闻语言重在传播新闻事实。而新闻语言的主要特点是准确贴切、简洁明快、生动形象，这就促成新闻翻译的原则，即选词准确、语言通俗、文体适切、快速迅捷。新闻翻译以事实为基础，且具有庞大的受众群体，其语言的表达方式一定要准确无误，译者要准确表达事实，不得有任何虚假。新闻是要极短的时间内传播大量的信息，因此目的语要简洁易懂。

第二节 专业术语与常用表达

ST	TT
1.新型冠状病毒的主要亚型	major subtypes of novel coronavirus
2.输入性病例	imported novel coronavirus cases/ imported COVID-19 cases
3.(病毒感染)零新增	zero new infections
4.休舱	cabin hospital to suspend operation
5.抗疫国际合作	international cooperation on fighting the COVID-19 outbreak
6.重大突发公共卫生事件一级响应	first-level public health emergency response
7.数字化健康证明	digital health certificate
8.中、低风险地	medium-and low-risk areas
9.全国封锁	nationwide lockdown
10.医疗废物处置能力	medical waste disposal capacity
11.出入境防疫	epidemic prevention at borders
12.预约进站	reservation at subway stations
13.妨害国境卫生检疫罪	crime of disturbing frontier health and quarantine
14.行走的传染源	mobile source of infection
15.社区疫情防控	community-based epidemic prevention and control
16.一线工作人员	people who work on the front line
17.为基层减负	relieve burdens at the grassroots level
18.疫苗临床试验和上市使用	clinical reserve and application of vaccines
19.国家疫苗储备制度	national reserve system for vaccines
20.全面恢复生产生活秩序	comprehensively restore the order of production and life
21.复工复产	resumption of work and production
22.差异化精准防控策略	precise and differentiated epidemic control strategies
23.新时代中国青年	Chinese youth of the new era
24.新时代最可爱的人	the most admirable people in the new era

续表

ST	TT
25.草原生态保护修复	grassland ecological protection and restoration
26.湿地保护修复	wetland protection and restoration
27.奥林匹克圣火采集仪式	Olympics torch lighting ceremony
28.青铜天花板	bronze ceiling
29.城市绿地减少	urban creep
30.豆腐块式公园	pocket park
31.针对贫困家庭学生的优惠措施	preferential measures for impoverished students
32.社会救助兜底脱贫	strengthen social assistance to fight against poverty
33.贫困发生率	poverty headcount ratio
34.用眼疲劳	eyestrain
35.新职业	new professions
36.24小时网上校园招聘	24-hour online campus recruitment service
37.网上面试	conduct online interview
38.群面	group interview
39.网上签约	sign employment contract online
40.猎头	headhunt
41.劳动合同	labor contact
42.员工福利待遇	employee benefits package
43.公筷公勺	serving chopsticks and spoons
44.一客一用一消毒	disinfection after each serving
45.分餐制	serving of individual dishes
46.智能制造工程技术人员	intelligent manufacturing technicians
47.呼吸治疗师	respiratory therapists
48.网约配送员	delivery personnel for online orders
49.出生缺陷防控咨询师	birth defects prevention consultants
50.铁路综合维修工	railway general maintenance personnel

第三节　英译汉翻译实务

一、原文

The problem may be that sick-pay rules are too strict for employees, not too generous. Given the need to pay the rent, many low-paid workers may feel they have to work unless they are so sick as to be physically incapable of leaving the house. But things may be changing. In America the Democrats have long proposed statutory sick leave. President Donald Trump now talks of emergency relief for sick workers.

British policy has also shifted. Statutory sick pay will now be payable on the first day of absence, rather than the fourth. In its budget on March 11th the government removed a minimum income requirement that kept many part-time workers from qualifying for sick pay. It will also allow workers to get a sick note online rather than travel to a clinic and risk infecting other patients. Further change may still be needed. The statutory weekly rate, at £94.25 ($123), is less than 20% of average earnings, and may tempt more workers to turn up when feeling iffy.

二、学生译文初稿

问题可能在于，病假工资的规定对员工来说过于严格，而不是很宽松。考虑到需要支付房租，许多低收入工人可能会觉得自己必须工作，除非他们病得很重，以至于无法离开家里。但情况可能正在改变。在美国，民主党人早就提议设立法定病假。唐纳德•特朗普总统现在谈到了对于生病工人的紧急救济。

英国的政策也发生了变化。如今，法定病假工资将在工人缺勤的第一天支付，而不是第四天才支付。在3月11日的预算中，政府取消了一项最低收入要求，这使许多兼职工人失去了领取病假工资的资格。它还将允许工人在网上得到病假条，而不是冒着感染其他病人的风险去诊所。政策可能还需要进一步改变。法定每周的工资为94.25英镑（合123美元），低于平均收入的20%，这可能会导致更多的工人在感到不舒服时前来上班。

——译员：王鹏燕

三、学生译文修改稿

问题可能在于病假工资的规定对员工来说过于严格，显得不太宽松。考虑到需要支付房租，许多低收入工人可能会觉得自己必须工作，除非他们病得很重，以至于无法外出工作。但情况可能正在发生改变。在美国，民主党人长期以来一直提议设立法定病假。美国总统唐纳德·特朗普现在也谈到了为生病工人提供紧急救济的问题。

英国的政策也发生了变化。如今，工人在缺勤的第一天就会收到法定病假工资，而非第四天。在 3 月 11 日的预算中，政府取消了一项使许多兼职工人失去了领取病假工资资格的最低收入要求。此外，工人还可以在网上领取病假条，而不是冒着感染其他病人的风险去诊所。政府可能还需要进一步改变政策，因为工人的法定周薪为 94.25 英镑（合 123 美元），不到平均收入的 20%，这可能会导致更多的工人在身体不适时去上班。

删除[杨]: ，

删除[杨]: 而不是很

删除[杨]: 离开家里

删除[杨]: 早就

删除[杨]: 总统

删除[杨]: 对于

删除[杨]: 的

删除[杨]: 法定病假工资将在工人缺勤的第一天支付，而不是第四天才支付

删除[杨]: 最低收入要求，这

删除[杨]: 的

删除[杨]: 它还将允许

删除[杨]: 得到

删除[杨]: 政策

删除[杨]: 。

删除[杨]: 每周的工资

删除[杨]: 低于

删除[杨]: 感到不舒服时前来

审校：张静&杨雯

时间：2020.04.04

四、学生译文终稿

问题可能在于病假工资的规定对员工来说过于严格，显得不太宽松。考虑到需要支付房租，许多低收入工人可能会觉得自己必须工作，除非他们病得很重，以至于无法外出工作。但情况可能正在发生改变。在美国，民主党人长期以来一直提议设立法定病假。美国总统唐纳德•特朗普现在也谈到了为生病工人提供紧急救济的问题。

英国的政策也发生了变化。如今，工人在缺勤的第一天就会收到法定病假工资，而非第四天。在3月11日的预算中，政府取消了一项使许多兼职工人失去了领取病假工资资格的最低收入要求。此外，工人还可以在网上领取病假条，而不是冒着感染其他病人的风险去诊所。政府可能还需要进一步改变政策，因为工人的法定周薪为94.25英镑（合123美元），不到平均收入的20%，这可能会导致更多的工人在身体不适时去上班。

审校员：张静&杨雯

审校时间:2020.3.7

五、参考译文

问题根源可能在于带薪病假的规定太过苛刻，不够慷慨。为了付房租，很多低收入者除非病到不能出门，还是会坚持上班。但形势或有好转。美国民主党派一直呼吁将病假写进联邦法律，美国总统特朗普也已提到要为生病员工提供紧急救济。

英国政策也有所转变。病假工资将依法从请假第一天开始计算，而不是第四天。3月11日，政府在年度预算中移除了曾让很多兼职员工无权享受带薪病假的最低收入要求。此外，开具病假条也无需去诊所,员工在线申请即可，以免疾病传染他人。但政策可能还需进一步调整。目前法定的病假周薪为94.25英镑(约合人民币808元),不足平均工资的20%，这可能致使员工即使身体抱恙还会坚持上班。

第四节　汉译英翻译实务

一、原文

为防止食源性疾病传播，进一步守护消费者健康，北京烹饪协会、北京市餐饮行业协会联合倡议北京餐饮行业推行公筷公勺行动。

倡议号召，本市餐饮服务要配备公筷公勺，有条件的企业可定制带有“公”字标识的公筷公勺；严格做好公筷公勺清洗、消毒，设置公筷公勺专用存放区；根据餐桌规格、用餐人数、菜品类型等，摆放相应的公筷公勺；火锅等必须在餐桌熟制的餐饮服务，应提供专用“生料公筷”；自助餐厅或由消费者自行取餐的餐厅，配置与菜品相对应的公筷公勺。

二、学生译文初稿

To prevent the spread of food–borne diseases and further protect the healthof consumers, the Beijing Cuisine Association and the Beijing Catering Industry Association jointly advocate the Beijing Catering Industry to implement serving chopsticks and spoons initiative.

The initiative calls for catering services in this city to be equipped with serving chopsticks and spoons. Qualified enterprises can equip with the chopsticks with the "serving" logo; strictly wash and disinfect the serving chopsticks and set up special serving chopsticks and spoons storage areas; place corresponding serving chopsticksand spoons inaccordance with table specifications, number of diners, type of dishes, etc; hot pots and other catering services that must be cooked at the table, special "raw chopsticks" should be provided; buffet restaurants or the self–catering restaurant is equipped with serving chopsticks and spoons corresponding to the dishes.

——译员：陈春

三、学生译文修改稿

In order to prevent the spread of food-borne diseases and further protect the health of consumers, the Beijing Cuisine Association and the Beijing Catering Industry Association jointly proposed the implementation of the action of serving chopsticks and spoons in the Beijing catering industry.

The proposal calls for catering services in this city to be equipped with serving chopsticks and spoons. Qualified enterprises can customize the public chopsticks with the "public" logo; strictly clean and disinfect the serving chopsticks and spoon as well as set up special storage areas; according to table specifications, , number of diners, type of dishes, etc , place corresponding serving chopsticks and spoons; hot pots and other catering services that must be cooked at the table, special "raw chopsticks" should be provided; buffet restaurants or the self-catering restaurant shall be equipped with serving chopsticks and spoons corresponding to the dishes.

删除[A]: To

删除[A]: advocate

删除[A]: to implement

删除[A]: servering

删除[A]: spoons

删除[A]: initiative

删除[乔]: initiative

删除[A]: equip

删除[A]: with

删除[A]: serving

删除[A]: wash

删除[A]: and

删除[A]: place corresponding serving chopsticks and spoons

删除[A]: etc.

审校员：何丽霞

审校时间:2020.04.04

四、学生译文终稿

In order to prevent the spread of food-borne diseases and further protect the health of consumers,the Beijing Cuisine Association and the Beijing Catering Industry Association jointly proposed the implementation of the action of serving chopsticks and spoons in the Beijing catering industry.

The proposal calls for catering services in this city to be equipped with serving chopsticks and spoons. Qualified enterprises can customize the public chopsticks with the "public" logo; strictly clean and disinfect the serving chopsticks and spoon as well as set up special storage areas; according to table specifications,number of diners, type of dishes, etc; place corresponding serving chopsticks and spoons; hot pots and other catering services that must be cooked at the table, special "raw chopsticks" should be provided; buffet restaurants or the self-catering restaurant shall be equipped with serving chopsticks and spoons corresponding to the dishes.

审校员：何丽霞

审校时间：2020.3.7

五、参考译文

In order to prevent the spread of food-borne diseases, the Beijing Cuisine Association and the Beijing Food and Beverage Industry Association jointly launched a campaign to promote the use of serving chopsticks and spoons across Beijing's catering industry.

According to the initiative, the city's dining venues should provide diners with common serving chopsticks and spoons, thoroughly clean and disinfected, stored in designated storage area. According to the new dining safety measure, number of diners, the type of dishes, put the corresponding serving chopsticks and spoons for each dish. Hot pot and other dishes that are cooked at the table should have special chopsticks for the raw ingredients. Cafeterias need to provide serving chopsticks and spoons for each dish.

第五节　翻译实务评析

一、词法分析

汉语追求话语表达的简单凝练，原文（英译汉）中，"low-paid workers"并未直译为“低收入工人”，而是“低收入者”。汉语是意合语言，应通过上下文语境体现其逻辑关系。例如：原文（英译汉）“But things may be changing”中的“things”根据上下文将具有复数含义的“诸多事情”译为更贴合原文的“形势”。汉语名词本身即可表达单数概念，又可表达复数概念，而英语不同，其名词复数可通过词形变化体现数的概念。例如：原文（汉译英）中，“本市餐饮服务要配备公筷公勺”，虽未明确公筷公勺的数量，但译文依常理将其译为“common serving chopsticks and spoons”。

二、句法分析

汉语对句式结构没有限定，无主语或多主语均可完整表达准确含义。而在英语中，除并列主谓以外，大多句子只包含一个主语和谓语。例如：原文（英译汉）中，“倡议号召，本市餐饮服务要配备公筷公勺，有条件的企业可定制带有‘公’字标识的公筷公勺。”三个短句有三个不同的主语，而在译文（汉译英）中，将“本市餐饮服务”定为主语后，借助介词短语将原文中的动词“号召”名词化。在表达多个定语时，汉语主要借助并列句，按照一定的时间和主次顺序，由浅至深，由弱至强，而英语常用长难句及复杂句。例如：原文（汉译英）中，五个具体防疫措施以四个分号符号分隔，译文中将其整合为四个完整的句子。

三、语篇分析

衔接和连贯是语篇分析的重要方面，译文通顺且逻辑分明是对译文的基本要求。因此，要使译文行文连贯，衔接词、转折语必不可少。在翻译中，若直译使原文意义不明或冗余时，译者应根据实际情况，采取增词，省词等方法，使译文衔接连贯。例如：原文（英译汉）第二段中，列举了多种解决目前困难的具体举措，却没有任何表示顺序衔接的标志词汇，因此译者在翻译过程中加入了“此外”一词，简洁明了地提出另一种解决办法。新闻播报往往讲究用词的简洁，所以短词、缩略词居多。例如：原文（英译汉）中，“为防止食源性疾病传播，进一步守护消费者健康，北京烹饪协会、北京市餐饮行业协会联合倡议北京餐饮行业推行公筷公勺行动”，本句的重点在于“推行公筷公勺行动”，且“进一步守护消费者健康”与前一句意义相似，因此译者采用省译法。

【课外拓展】

请选取不同题材的新闻报道，与你的团队模拟英语主持人现场新闻播报的情境。

文献参考

[1]冯全功,李嘉伟．新闻翻译的译后编辑模式研究[J]．外语电化教学,2016(06):74-79.

[2]黄忠廉．翻译项目管理[M]．北京:国防工业出版社,2014.

[3]廖志勤．英文新闻标题及其翻译策略[J]．中国科技翻译,2006(02):44-47.

[4]梁满玲,胡伟华．外媒"洪荒之力"英译的"全球本土化"解读[J]．上海翻译,2017(06):38-42.

[5]钱叶萍,王银泉．从功能翻译理论看软新闻的汉译英[J]．北京第二外国语学院学报,2006(06):11-14.

[6]孙毅,孟林林．认知术语学视角下的外交部网站新闻术语翻译[J]．上海翻译,2018(04):30-38.

[7]孙毅,曾昕,郝学宏．项目管理模式理论视阈下外交新闻翻译实践述略[J]．上海翻译,2016(06):75-82+94.

[8]徐英．机构新闻翻译情境下情态选择的编译改动与意识形态的转换[J]．外语教学,2018,39(03):93-97.

[9]徐英．新闻编译中意识形态的翻译转换探索[J]．中国翻译,2014,35(03):98-102.

[10]张美芳．翻译中的超文本成分:以新闻翻译为例[J]．中国翻译,2011,32(02):50-55.

第八章 体育翻译

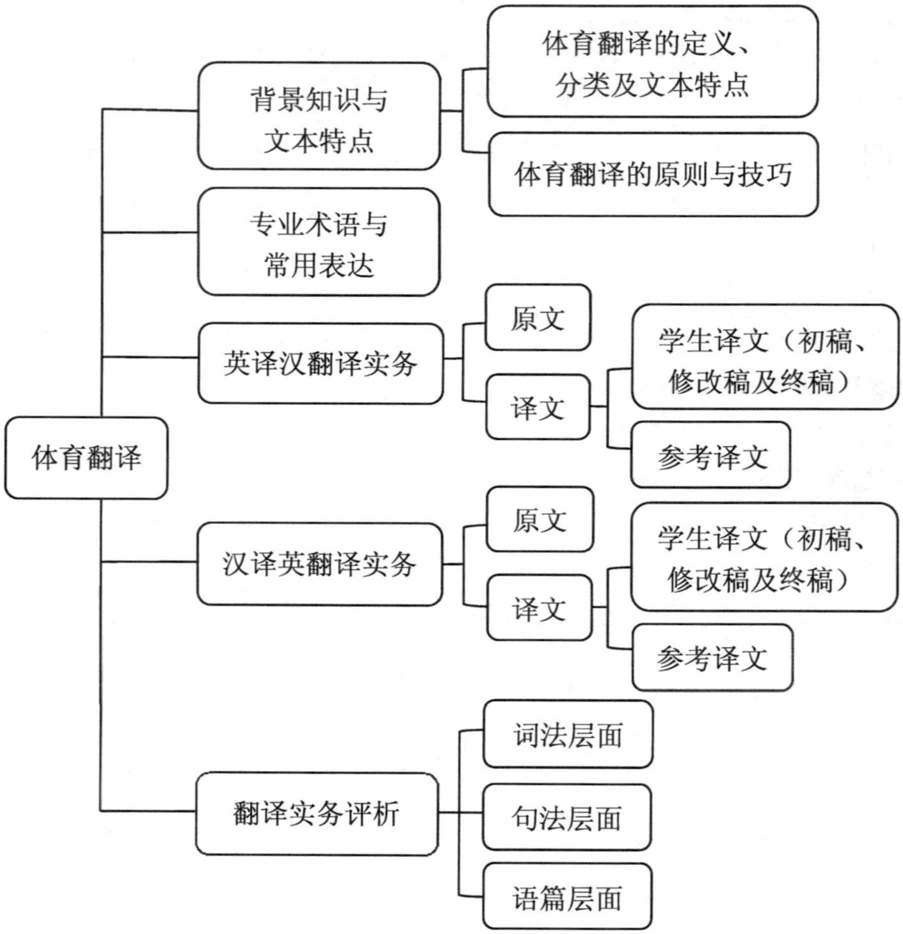
体育翻译
背景知识与文本特点
体育翻译的定义、分类及文本特点
体育翻译的原则与技巧
专业术语与常用表达
英译汉翻译实务
原文
译文
学生译文（初稿、修改稿及终稿）
参考译文
汉译英翻译实务
原文
译文
学生译文（初稿、修改稿及终稿）
参考译文
翻译实务评析
词法层面
句法层面
语篇层面

第一节　背景知识与文本特点

一、体育翻译定义、分类及文本特点

体育翻译究其根源属于特殊应用型文本翻译，即对体育相关的文本类型的语言转换，包括体育新闻口译和笔译、体育网站翻译、体育影视翻译、体育用品翻译、体育陪同翻译等。从广义上来看，体育英语就是在一切与体育相关的活动中使用的具有特殊表达形式的语言变体。从狭义上来看，体育英语就是在体育赛事或体育活动中使用英语作为交际工具的语言，具有其特殊性。体育翻译主要以宣传为主，涵盖不同翻译项目，体现的是不同文化间的交流。在用词方面，体育类文本大量使用专业术语、缩略语和合成词，如国际足联（国际足球联合会）译为FIFA（Federation Internationale de Football Association），季后赛则译为“playoff”。在句法方面，体育类文本句子简短，多使用简单句和感叹句且表现力十足，如“扬体育精神，展青春风采”可翻译为“promote the spirit of sports and develop the youth”。在修辞方面，体育类文本多综合使用夸张，暗喻等多种修辞手法，如2020年东京奥运会口号“United by Emotion”，新华社译为“激情聚会”，不同领域的学者用不同的修辞手法译出了各自的风格。

二、体育翻译的原则与技巧

译者的翻译行为应遵循文本特征与翻译目的。对于翻译原则与技巧的选择也必须视文本的特殊性而定。体育翻译的目的在于准确传递原文信息。其翻译原则是准确性原则和可读性原则。首先，此类文本用词新奇、专业词汇丰富。专业术语和特定词汇在体育翻译中至关重要。译者在翻译时应当查阅相关的工具书或借助网络等方法准确地表达出原文的意思。基于这一特征，译者在翻译的过程中应充分考虑文本中所含的专有名词及其他常用词汇，需采用省略、增词、直译、词类转换等翻译原则与技巧，在确保译文准确性的基础上忠实于原文内容。其次，体育类文本句子结构十分紧凑、简短而富有张力，多用感叹句和陈述句。因此，译者在翻译时应当采用顺序法、逆序法、分译法和综合法等翻译方法，同时要充分考虑句型结构和内容表达。此外，体育翻译要根据语境适当地变通或删减信息，最大限度地保持译文通俗易懂、简明顺畅，使译文有较强的感染力，可以将读者带入目的语语境中。总的来说，体育类文本有自身独特的文体特征，只有准确把握原文所表达的信息及其文本特征，才能使目的语读者准确理解原文，保证读者获取到准确无误的信息。体育翻译中译员应充分掌握这些技巧，用地道的语言翻译体育文本，使文本内容更加清晰明确，从而达到翻译目的。

第二节　专业术语与常用表达

ST	TT
1.国际奥林匹克委员会	IOC(International Olympic Committee)
2.击剑	epee fencing
3.射击	pistol shooting
4.越野跑	cross-country running
5.低于标准杆	under par
6.国际田联(国际田径联合会)	IAAF(International Association of Athletics Federations)
7.国际足联(国际足球联合会)	FIFA(Federation Internationale de Football Association)
8.季后赛	Playoff
9.蝶泳	butterfly stroke
10.全明星赛	all-stars game
11.抽签	Draw
12.夺冠	Claim the title
13.竞技体育	Competitive Sports
14.职业体育	Professional Sports
15.群众体育	Mass Sports
16.自由泳	Freestyle
17.全民健身运动	National fitness campaign
18.国际军事体育理事会	CISM
19.世界军人运动会	Military World Games

续表

ST	TT
20.奥林匹克圣歌	Olympic Hymn/Anthem
21.奥林匹克体育场	Olympic Stadium
22.奥运会主场地	Main Olympic Venue
23.奥运火炬塔	Olympic cauldron
24.奥运火炬	Olympic torch
25.火炬手	Torch bearer
26.火炬接力	Torch relay
27.残疾奥运会	Special Olympics/Paralympics
28.国家体育总局	State Sport General Administration
29.核心队员	backbone player/lead man
30.结束比赛	wrap up the games
31.隆重闭幕	close with a bang
32.七连冠	Seven-time defending champion
33.全能选手	all- rounder
34.绕场一周向观众致意	Undertake laps of honor
35.申办城市	bidding city
36.世界杯马拉松比赛	World Marathon Cup
37.世界大学生运动会	Universiade
38.世界锦标赛	World championships
39.刷新纪录	rewrite/renew the world's record
40.现场直播	live broadcast
41.亚洲运动会	Asian Games
42.中华全国体育总会	All-China Sports Federation
43.冠军杯(冠军联赛)	Champions League

续表

ST	TT
44.欧洲杯	Euro Cup
45.内定比赛结果，比赛造假	match fixing
46.罚点球决胜	penalty shoot-out
47.将比分拉开	pull away / widen the gap
48.为体育队加油	root for the team
49.激烈竞争	tug-of-war
50.反败为胜	turn the tide/ turn the table

第三节　英译汉翻译实务

一、原文

Parachuting is a method of transiting from a high point to the earth with the aid of gravity, involving the control of speed during the descent with the use of a parachute or parachutes. Parachuting in Military World Games involves 18 events in three categories: accuracy, overall and formation skydiving.

The PLA Bayi parachuting team has won more than 300 championships since its establishment in 1958. It has also been awarded the honorary title of The Sports Team that Climbs to the Peak by the State General Administration of Sport. The training of parachuters also has a practical significance for empowering the airborne troops.

二、学生译文初稿

跳伞是借助重力从高空到地面的一种方法，包括使用降落伞或降落伞在下降过程中控制速度。世界军事运动会的跳伞包括三个类别的18个项目:精确跳伞、整体跳伞和编队跳伞。

解放军八一跳伞队自1958年成立以来，已经获得了300多次冠军。它还被国家体育总局授予“登顶运动队”荣誉称号。跳伞人员的训练对增强空降部队的战斗力也具有现实意义。

——译员：王婷婷

三、学生译文修改稿

这项极限运动大家应该都不陌生，在军运会赛场上，跳伞是借助重力从高空到地面的一种方法，借助空气动力和降落伞，包括使用降落伞或降落伞在下降过程中完成规定动作，并利用降落伞减缓下降速度，在指定区域安全着陆。世界军事运动会的跳伞包括三个类别:精确跳伞、整体跳伞和编队跳伞，共产生 18 枚金牌

删除[y]：控制速度

删除[y]：的 18 个项目

删除[y]：。

解放军八一跳伞队是这几个军队中历史最悠久的了，自 1958 年成立以来，已经获得了 300 多项冠军。曾被国家体育总局授予"勇攀高峰运动队"荣誉称号。跳伞人员的训练对增强空降部队的战斗力也具有很强的实战意义。

删除[y]：次

删除[y]：它还

删除[y]：登顶

删除[y]：现实

审校员：张云燕

审校时间：2020.3.10

四、学生译文终稿

这项极限运动大家应该都不陌生，在军运会赛场上，跳伞是借助重力从高空到地面的一种方法，借助空气动力和降落伞，包括使用降落伞或降落伞在下降过程中完成规定动作，并利用降落伞减缓下降速度，在指定区域安全着陆。世界军事运动会的跳伞包括三个类别:精确跳伞、整体跳伞和编队跳伞，共产生18枚金牌。

解放军八一跳伞队是这几个军队中历史最悠久的了，自1958年成立以来，已经获得了300多项冠军。它还曾被国家体育总局授予“勇攀高峰运动队”荣誉称号。跳伞人员的训练对增强空降部队的战斗力也具有很强的实战意义。

审校员：张云燕

审校时间:2020.3.7

五、参考译文

这项极限运动大家应该都不陌生，在军运会赛场上，运动员乘飞机升至高空然后跳下，借助空气动力和降落伞，在降落伞张开前后完成规定动作，并利用降落伞减缓下降速度，在指定区域安全着陆。军运会的跳伞分为三大项：定点跳

伞、特技跳伞和造型跳伞，共产生18枚金牌。

我军的跳伞队是这几个军体队中历史最悠久的了，1958年组建以来，已经获得了300多项冠军，曾被原国家体委授予“勇攀高峰运动队”荣誉称号，跳伞队员的培养为我军空降兵的兵力方面也有很强的实战意义。

第四节 汉译英翻译实务

一、原文

军事五项1946年由法国军官提议创立，堪称军运会中最精彩，也是最艰苦，最锻炼军人素质的项目。五项指的是：射击、障碍跑、障碍游泳、投弹和越野跑，所比拼的素质技能都是陆军单兵战斗的必备技能，非常贴合现代部队作战。

世界军事五项锦标赛更是军体理事会举办届次最多的赛事。根据参赛者5项比赛总成绩确定名次，本届运动会共设男女个人、团体和障碍跑接力6枚金牌。

军事五项也是我们中国队比较有实力的项目之一。这届军运会上，6枚金牌中国队斩获了5枚。

二、学生译文初稿

The military pentathlon initiated by French officers in 1946, which are the most exciting, the most arduous and the most soldier-oriented events in the military Games. The military pentathlon include shooting, obstacle running, obstacle swimming, bombing, and cross-country running. The qualities and skills that are required for individual combat in the army are well suited to modern army operations.

The World Military Pentathlon Championship is the most held by the CMC. There will be 6 gold MEDALS for men and women in individual, team and obstacle relay, according to the overall results of the 5 events.

Military Pentathlon is also one of the more powerful items of our Chinese team. China won five of the six gold MEDALS at the games.

——译员：牛婷

三、学生译文修改稿

The idea of organizing a sports competition exclusively for the army was proposed in 1946 by a French officer. It is known as the most spectacular event but also the toughest, requiring high military qualities. It contains five races: shooting, obstacle run, obstacle swimming, throwing and cross country.

The Military Pentathlon World Championships are the most regular event held by CISM. Contestants are ranked based on all five scores combined and the games contain six gold medals from men and women's individual, team and obstacle relay.

The military pentathlon is also one of the more powerful items in which China has some strengths. The Chinese military pentathlon won five out of the six gold medals in this year's games.

删除[y]: World

删除[y]: is

删除[y]: CMC

删除[y]: M

删除[y]: P

删除[y]: of our Chinese team

删除[y]: China

删除[y]: MEDALS

删除[y]: at the

审校员：张云燕

审校时间：2020.3.10

四、学生译文终稿

The idea of organizing a sports competition exclusively for the army was proposed in 1946 by a French officer. It is known as the most spectacular event but also the toughest, requiring high military qualities. It contains five races: shooting, obstacle run, obstacle swimming, throwing and cross country.

The Military Pentathlon World Championships are the most regular event held by CISM. Contestants are ranked based on all five scores combined and the games contain six gold medals from men and women′s individual, team and obstacle relay.

The military pentathlon is also one of the more powerful items which China has some strengths. The Chinese military pentathlon won five out of the six gold medalsin this year′s games.

审校员：张云燕

审校时间：2020.3.7

五、参考译文

The idea of organizing a sports competition exclusively for the army was proposed in 1946 by a French officer. It is known as the most spectacular event but also the toughest, requiring high military qualities. It contains five races: shooting, obstacle run, obstacle swimming, throwing and cross country.

The Military Pentathlon World Championships are also the most regular event organized by CISM. Contestants are ranked based on all five scores combined and the games contain six gold medals from men and women's individual, team and obstacle relay.

The military pentathlon is also one of the military sports in which China has some strengths. The Chinese military pentathlon team pocketed five out of all six gold medals in this year'sgames.

第五节 翻译实务评析

一、词法分析

专业术语和特定词汇的大量运用是体育文本的鲜明特色。例如原文（英译汉）中出现的相关专业词汇："Parachuting"（跳伞）、"Military World Games"（军运会）、"The Sports Team that Climbs to the Peak"（勇攀高峰运动队）、"the State General Administration of Sport"（国家体育总局）和"airborne troops"（空降部队）等，其正确翻译体现了译员充分的译前准备工作和扎实的知识储备，增强了体育翻译的专业性。

二、句法分析

体育文本句子结构紧凑，简短而富有张力。在翻译过程中，一般常用直译、意译和增译法。例如，原文（英译汉）第一句，学生译文在翻译过程中过于直译，使得译文死板僵硬。反观参考译文，译者采用了增译法，在这句话前面增添了背景信息："这项极限运动大家应该都不陌生，在军运会赛场上……"既保证了译文结构的完整性又准确传递了译文的信息。原文（英译汉）第二段整体采用了直译法，但为了使译文内容更为饱满，依旧结合了增译法，例如："The PLA Bayi parachuting team has won more than 300 championships since its establishment in 1958."参考译文进行了修饰补充，最终译为"解放军八一跳伞队是这几个军队中历史最悠久的了……。”此外，原文（汉译英）第一句“军事五项1946年由法国军官提议创立，堪称军运会中最精彩，也是最艰苦，最锻炼军人素质的项目。”学生译文处理为主句加非限制性定语从句的形式，译为“The military pentathlon initiated by French officers in 1946, which are the most exciting, the most arduous and the most soldier-oriented events in the military Games.”生成的译文较为生硬，但参考译文译者将“军事五项”译为“a sports competition”，并且做了短句处理，将原句进行拆分重组，体现了汉语重意合而英语重形合的特点，且遵循了“信”和“达”的翻译原则。

三、语篇分析

不同于其他应用类文本，体育文本具有特殊的语篇结构。在具体语篇中，句与句之间不是机械的组合，而是意义上的有机整合，不仅具有意义上的相关性，而且具有形式上的同一性。例如：原文（英译汉）第二段前两句中，“its”和“It”均指代“The PLA Bayi parachuting team”（解放军八一跳伞队），此处代词连贯衔接语篇语义，层次分明，实现了语篇结构的严密性。例如：原文（汉译英）第一段，“军事五项”译为“a sports competition”，译文第二、三句中的“It”也都指代前一句的“军事五项”，既忠实于原文又着重体现了原文的连贯性与完整性，便于目的语读者理解和接受。

【课外拓展】

某国际运动会邀请你担任现场赛事解说的翻译，请模拟情境进行表演。

文献参考

[1]陈其嘉．英语体育新闻的特点及其翻译技巧[D]．上海外国语大学，2009．

[2]何蓉．功能对等理论下体育广告的翻译策略研究[J]．兰州教育学院学报，2016，32(04)：152-153．

[3]黄佳丽．功能翻译理论视角下的体育新闻导语英译[D]．广东外语外贸大学，2008．

[4]黄忠廉．翻译项目管理[M]．北京：国防工业出版社，2014．

[5]罗永洲．体育文本的类型与翻译探析[J]．中国翻译，2012，33(04)：104-107．

[6]孟莲芬,韦建军. 体育翻译中词义的选择[J]. 上海科技翻译,1997(04):15-18.

[7]王彬. 文化视阈下体育新闻中隐喻的翻译[J]. 中国科技翻译,2008(03):55-57+65.

[8]袁彬. 语言学翻译理论视角下的体育英语翻译研究[J]. 成都体育学院学报,2019,45(01):73-79.

[9]杨飞."ESP"理论视角下的大型国际赛事体育英语翻译现状分析[J]. 成都体育学院学报,2015,41(03):64-67.

第九章　法律翻译

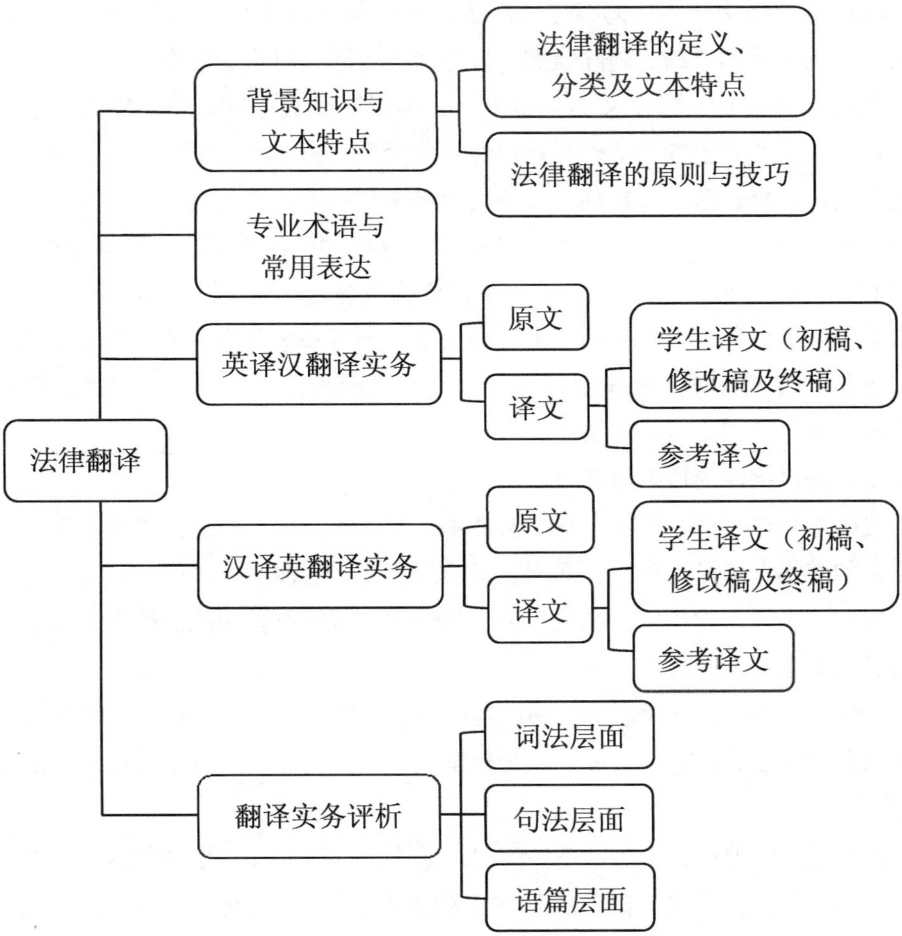
法律翻译
背景知识与文本特点
法律翻译的定义、分类及文本特点
法律翻译的原则与技巧
专业术语与常用表达
英译汉翻译实务
原文
译文
学生译文（初稿、修改稿及终稿）
参考译文
汉译英翻译实务
原文
译文
学生译文（初稿、修改稿及终稿）
参考译文
翻译实务评析
词法层面
句法层面
语篇层面

第一节　背景知识与文本特点

一、法律翻译定义、分类及文本特点

法律翻译即法律文件的翻译，而法律文件所含的内容很广泛，包括：法律、法规、条约、国际公约、国际惯例、涉外经济合同、司法文书等。

从词汇层面看，法律文本多用术语，用以准确表达特有法律概念；多用古语，以增加法律英语的神圣性和权威性；多用正式语，从而增加法律文本的庄重规范的文体风格；多用外来词，其中主要是来自拉丁语和法语词汇；多用成对词（如：terms and conditions 指“条款和条件”,这些词的结构固定，有固定的意义，使用和翻译时不能随意拆开）。法律文件作为具有法律效力的特殊性文本，语言要求高度准确，用词需要字斟句酌，而文本自身有一些基本特征，其文本更为正式、刻板、专业性强，句子长而复杂，用词准确规范，语篇结构严谨，逻辑性强，多有规范的固定格式和用语。

二、法律翻译的原则与技巧

法律翻译要研究、掌握在法律文件中的文本语言特点，在准确的基础上，做好语言的转换，使译入语达到通顺、优美的程度。法律文件中的英语具有用词准确、规范，多用法律用语，结构严谨，长句构造等特点。因此法律文件的翻译一般遵循以下原则：

1. 精确性原则：法律语言的高度精确性要求同样适用于法律文本的翻译，法律文书正式程度较高，涉及面广，责任重大，因此精确性原则是法律翻译的至高准则；

2. 正式性原则：法律语言是各国的正式语言，法律文本是法律内容和法律效果的载体，其责任重大，在选词上必须采用规范化，正式化的书面语，要注意其行文风格，以体现法律文件的正式庄严特色；

3. 创造性原则：中西语言文化上有差异，其政治制度，法律体系也有所不同，译员要借助其娴熟的语际转换能力和准确的认知能力，要发挥一定的创造性使原文与译文在内容和法律效果两方面都达到对等。

此外，针对法律文本具体可运用的翻译技巧有：法律翻译要注意词义的变换和语序的调整；充分考虑增词和减词的情况；出现从句时按照原文的顺序翻译即可，但有时也要根据上下文的意思适当调整语序，以体现法律文本的逻辑关系。

第二节　专业术语与常用表达

ST	TT
1.案件受理费	court acceptance fee
2.案件陈述书	statement of case
3.案由	cause of action
4.办案人员	personnel handling a case
5.辩护律师	defense attorney / lawyer
6.不公开审理	trial in camera
7.不可抗力	force majeure
8.罚款	impose a fine
9.道德退化	morally degraded
10.道德责任	moral obligation
11.法律意识	legal awareness
12.法律援助	legal aid
13.个人信用体系	personal credit system
14.公证机关	public notary office
15.国际诉讼	international litigation
16.监护责任	liability of guardian
17.监控录像	security-camera footage
18.检察权	prosecutorial power
19.经济审判庭	economic tribunal
20.开庭审理	open a court session
21.看守所	detention house
22.扣分处罚	point penalty
23.挪用公款	misappropriate public funds
24.派出所	police station / office
25.司法部	Ministry of Justice

续表

ST	TT
26.司法机关	judicial organs
27.法律文件	Legal documents
28.双边协议	bilateral agreements
29.人权	human rights
30.虚拟身份	virtual identity
31.点击欺诈	click fraud
32.全球性勒索软件攻击	Global ransomware attack
33.立案	File a case
34.共同打击跨国犯罪	Jointly combat transnational crimes
35.占道经营	Roadside booths
36.出口退税机制	The mechanism for export tax rebates
37.保护主义	Protectionism
38.拘役	Criminal detention, from one month to six months
39.有期徒刑	Fixed-term imprisonment
40.无期徒刑	Non-fixed-term imprisonment
41.死刑	Death penalty
42.犯罪要件	Elements of a crime
43.犯罪主体	Subject
44.犯罪客体	Object
45.正当防卫	Self- defense
46.共同犯罪	Complicity in an offense
47.共犯	Principal
48.从犯	Accessory
49.信访举报	Letters, visits and whistleblowing
50.严打斗争	Strike-hard operation

第三节　英译汉翻译实务

一、原文

The Senate of the United States shall be composed of two Senators from each State, chosen by the Legislature thereof, for six years; and each Senate shall have one vote.

The legislature shall provide for the maintenance and support of a system of free common schools, wherein all the children of this state may be educated.

The protection and promotion of the health of the health of the inhabitants of the state are matters of public concern and provision therefor shall be made by the state and by such its subdivisions.

The legislature shall, by general law, conform all charters of savings banks, savings and loan associations, or institutions for savings, to a uniformity of powers, rights and liabilities, and all charters hereafter granted for such corporations shall be made to conform to such general law, and to such amendments thereto as may be made.

In case of the removal of the President from office, or of his death, resignation, or inability to discharge the powers and duties of the said office, the same shall devolve on the Vice-President, and the Congress may be law provide for the case of removal, death, resignation, or inability, both of the President and Vice-President, declaring what officer shall then act as President, as and such officer shall act accordingly until the disability be removed or a President shall be elected.

二、学生译文初稿

美国参议院由各州立法机构选举产生的两名参议员组成，任期六年，每一参议院有一票表决权。

立法机关应规定维持和支持一个免费的普通学校制度，在这一制度下，本州所有儿童都可以接受教育。

保护和促进国家居民的健康是公众关心的问题，由国家及其分支机构作出规定。

立法机构应依普通法，使储蓄银行、储蓄及贷款协会或储蓄机构的所有章程，符合权力、权利及法律责任的统一，而其后为该等公司批出的所有章程，均须符合该等普通法及对该等章程所做的修订。

如果总统被免职、或其死亡、辞职或不能履行上述职务的权力和职责，则应将此权力和职责移交给副总统，国会可通过法律规定总统和副总统的免职、死亡、辞职或不能履行职责的情况，宣布则该人员须以主席身份行事，而该人员须据此行事，直至该残疾人士被免职或选出主席为止。

——译员：张胜霞

三、学生译文修改稿

美国参议院应由各州立法机构选举产生的两名参议员组成，任期6年，每一参议院有一票表决权。

立法机关应规定维持和支持公立学校教育系统;在这一制度下，本州所有儿童都可以接受教育。

删除[T]：一个免费的普通学校制度

保护和促进本州居民的健康是公众关心的问题，由国家及其分支机构作出规定。

删除[T]：国家

立法机构应依通用法，使储蓄银行、储蓄及贷款协会或储蓄机构的所有章程，符合职权、权利及债务责任的统一，而其后为该公司批出的所有章程，均须符合该通用法及修改文件。

删除[T]：普通

删除[T]：权力

删除[T]：法律

删除[T]：等普通

删除[T]：对该等章程所作的修订

如果总统被免职、死亡、辞职或不能履行上述职务的权力和职责，则应将此权力和职责移交给副总统，国会可通过法律规定总统和副总统的免职、死亡、辞职或不能履行职责的情况，宣布由哪个官员来代理行使总统的权利与职责，在上述情况结束或新总统产生前，该官员应以总统身份行事。

删除[T]：或其

删除[T]：则该

删除[T]：人员

删除[T]：须以主席身分行事，而该人员须据此行事，直至该残疾人士被免职或选出主席为止。

审校员：何丽霞

审校时间：2020.3.7

四、学生译文终稿

美国参议院应由各州立法机构选举产生的两名参议员组成，任期6年，每一参议员有一票表决权。

立法机构应规定维持和支持公立学校教育系统；在这一制度下，本州所有儿童都可以接受教育。

保护和促进本州居民的健康是公众关心的问题，由国家及其分支机构作出规定。

立法机构应依通用法，使储蓄银行、储蓄及贷款协会或储蓄机构的所有章程，符合职权、权利及债务责任的统一，而其后为该公司批出的所有章程，均须符合该通用法及修改文件。

如果总统被免职、死亡、辞职或不能履行上述职务的权力和职责，则应将此权力和职责移交给副总统，国会可通过法律规定总统和副总统的免职、死亡、辞职或不能履行职责的情况，宣布由哪个官员来代理行使总统的权力与职责，在上述情况结束或新总统产生前，该官员应以总统身份行事。

审校员：何丽霞

审校时间:2020.3.7

五、参考译文

美国参议院应由每州两名参议员组成，参议员由各州立法机构选送，任期6年，每个参议员应有一个投票权。

州立法机构应立法规定，维护和支持免费就读的公立学校教育系统；本州的所有儿童都可在这类系统学校中受到教育。

保护、增强本州居民的健康是公众关注的问题。对本州居民健康的保护与增强的规定应由州及州下属机关作出。

州立法机构应根据通用法，使储蓄银行、储蓄与贷款协会、或储蓄机构的所有章程符合统一的职权、权利和债务责任，所有本宪法之后赋予上述存款机构的章程的制订都应符合上述通用法及通用法的修改文件。

如果总统免职、死亡、辞职或无能履行总统的权力与职责，应由副总统代理行使总统的权力与职责。国会可依法对总统和副总统的免职、死亡、辞职或无法履行的情况作出具体规定（提供法律依据），并宣布届时由哪个官员来代理行使总统的权力与职责，在上述无能履行情况结束前或新总统选举产生前，该官员应相应地代理行使权力与职责。

第四节　汉译英翻译实务

一、原文

当事人达成仲裁协议，一方向人民法院起诉的，人民法院不予受理，但仲裁协议无效的除外。

人民法院接到起诉状，经审查，应当在7日内定案或者作出裁定不予受理。原告对裁定不服的，可以提起上诉。

为了规范证券发行和交易行为，保护投资者的合法权益，维护社会经济秩序和社会公共利益，促进社会主义市场经济的发展，制定本法。

有限责任公司成立后设立分公司，应当有公司法定代表人向公司登记机关申请登记，领取营业执照。

二、学生译文初稿

If the parties reach an arbitration agreement and one party brings a lawsuit to the people's court, the people's court shall not accept it, unless the arbitration agreement is invalid.

The people's court shall, after examination, decide the case or make a ruling not to accept the complaint within 7 days after receiving it. If the plaintiff is not satisfied with the ruling, he may appeal.

This Law is formulated for the purpose of regulating the issuance and trading of securities, protecting the legitimate rights and interests of investors, maintaining social and economic order and public interests, and promoting the development of the socialist market economy.

When a branch company is established after the establishment of a limited liability company, the legal representative of the company shall apply to the company registration authority for registration and obtain a business license.

——译员：王婷婷

三、学生译文修改稿

A people's court shall not accept one party brings a lawsuit if the parties reach an arbitration agreement and one party brings a lawsuit to the people's court, unless arbitration agreement is invalid.

The people's court shall, after examination, file a case within 7 days or refuse the complaint after receiving it. If the plaintiff is not satisfied with the ruling decision, he may appeal against the court's decision.

This Law is formulated for the purpose of regulating the issuing and trading of securities, protecting the lawful rights and interests of investors, maintaining social and economic order and public interests, and promoting the development of the socialist market economy.

If a branch company is established after the establishment of a limited liability company, the legal representative of the company shall apply to the company registration authority for registration and obtain a business license.

删除[T]: If

删除[T]:

删除[T]: the people's court shall not accept it, unless the

删除[T]:

删除[T]: decide the

删除[T]: or make a ruling not to accept the complaint

删除[T]:

删除[T]: issuanc

删除[T]: e

删除[T]: -

删除[T]: legitimate

删除[T]: When

审校员：何丽霞

审校时间：2020.3.7

四、学生译文终稿

A people's court shall not accept one party brings a lawsuit if the parties reach an arbitration agreement and to the people's court, unless the arbitration agreement is invalid.

The people's court shall, upon examination, file a case within seven days or refuse the complaint after receiving it. If the plaintiff is not satisfied with the ruling decision, he may appeal against the court's decision.

This Law is formulated for the purpose of regulating the issuing and trading of securities, protecting the lawful rights and interests of investors, maintaining social and economic order and public interests, and promoting the development of the socialist market economy.

If a branch company is established after the establishment of a limited liability company, the legal representative of the company shall apply to the company registration authority for registration to obtain a business license.

审校员：何丽霞

审校时间：2020.3.7

五、参考译文

A people's court shall not accept an action initiated by either of the parties if the Parties have concluded and entered into an arbitration agreement, unless the arbitration agreement is invalid.

When a people's court receives a bill of complaint, the court in question shall, upon examination, file a case within seven days or decide to reject the complaint. If the plaintiff refuses to accept the decision made by the people's court, the plaintiff in question may appeal against the court's decision.

This Law is formulated and enacted in order to standardize the activities of issuing and trading securities, protect the lawful rights and interests of investors, safeguard the social economic order and social public interests and promote the development of the socialist market economy.

If, after the establishment of the company, a branch or branches of a limited company are established, the application for registration shall be made by the legal representative of company registration authorities to obtain the business licence（s）thereof.

第五节　翻译实务评析

一、词法分析

在翻译过程中，译者应在特定的语境中作出恰当的词汇选择。shall在陈述句中表示说话者的允诺、告诫、威胁、命令、必然性等，主要用于二、三人称，在法律、条约、协定等文件中表示义务、规定。例如，在英译汉中,每段都出现了

"shall"一词，译者在处理"shall"一词时，体现了法律条文的直接严谨。英语是表音文字，汉语是表意文字，因此在单复数处理方面有所差异。汉语名词不发生变化，是因其意象完整性和不可破坏性。因此在翻译时，应以英语形变代汉语意变。例如，在"当事人达成仲裁协议"一句中，当事人可能有多方，因而译者在翻译中，依情况而采用"parties"。

二、句法分析

被动语态的使用频次是英汉语言的显著差距，在英语中多出现被动语态，而汉语中被动语态较少，若出现被动语态，通常使用"受到""为……所……"等类似词汇体现被动构式。例如在"The Senate of the United States shall be composed of two Senators from each State, chosen by..."中，这句话为被动语态，汉译时，译者处理为主动语态，使译文更加符合译入语的行文规范，让目的语读者更好理解原文信息，明白其逻辑关系。在法律文本中，句子结构简明扼要，法律条文清晰，例如：英译汉第五段中，整句是长句，译者采取了直译法，遵循原文的语体特征和行文风格，体现出汉语重意合而英语重形合的语言特点。

三、语篇分析

法律翻译是一种法律转换和语言转换同时进行的双重工作，逻辑严谨，结构紧密，语篇内部衔接系统完整。由于法律文件具有高度的严肃性和严密性，这就要求译者在翻译实践中注重原文的完整性于一体性。例如：原文（英译汉）五段内容分别传递了不同类别的信息，但多次出现"also""and""wherein"等表示衔接关系的文字，因此，译者在翻译过程中忠实于原文，在译文中保留上述连词，从而体现文本的连贯性与整体性，也诠释了法律文件的严肃性和严密性。此外，代词的使用也是语篇逻辑性的重要体现。例如：原文（汉译英）"If the parties reach an arbitration agreement and one party brings a lawsuit to the people's court, the people's court shall not accept it"中"it"一词用来指代上文中所提及的法律条款，增强了上下文的衔接，用语严谨凝练。

【课外拓展】

请与你的团队就某民事案件进行模拟国际法庭的情境表演。

文献参考

[1]杜金榜．法律交流原则与法律翻译[J]．广东外语外贸大学学报，2005(04)：

11-14.

[2]杜金榜,张福,袁亮. 中国法律法规英译的问题和解决[J]. 中国翻译,2004(03):74-78.

[3]黄巍. 议法律翻译中译者的创造性[J]. 中国翻译,2002(02):40-42.

[4]黄忠廉. 翻译项目管理[M]. 北京:国防工业出版社,2014.

[5]金朝武,胡爱平. 试论我国当前法律翻译中存在的问题[J]. 中国翻译,2000(03):46-51.

[6]李德凤,胡牧. 法律翻译研究:现状与前瞻[J]. 中国科技翻译,2006(03):47-51.

[7]李克兴. 论法律文本的静态对等翻译[J]. 外语教学与研究,2010,42(01):59-65+81.

[8]张长明,仲伟合. 论功能翻译理论在法律翻译中的适用性[J]. 语言与翻译,2005(03):44-48.

[9]张法连. 法律英语翻译中的文化因素探析[J]. 中国翻译,2009,30(06):48-51+93.

[10]张法连. 法律文体翻译基本原则探究[J]. 中国翻译,2009,30(05):72-76.

[11]朱定初. 评复旦大学《法律英语》中的译注——兼谈法律专门术语翻译的基本原则[J]. 中国翻译,2002(03):67-72.

第十章 人物简介翻译

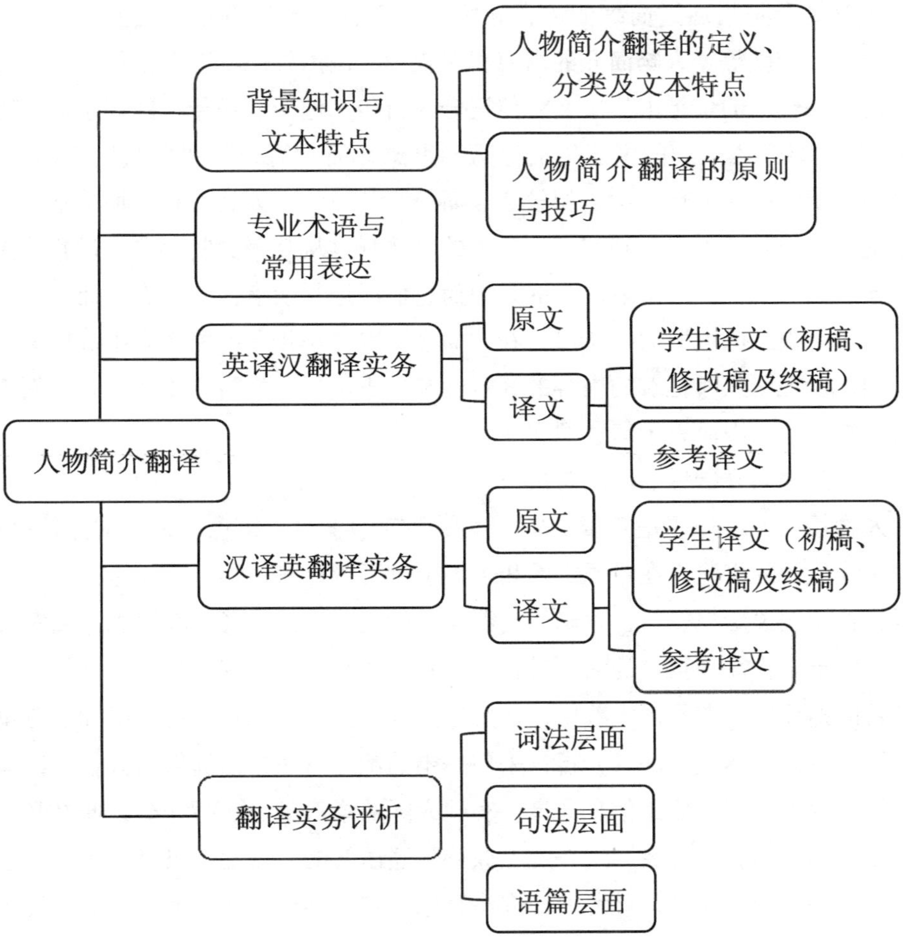
人物简介翻译
背景知识与文本特点
人物简介翻译的定义、分类及文本特点
人物简介翻译的原则与技巧
专业术语与常用表达
英译汉翻译实务
原文
译文
学生译文（初稿、修改稿及终稿）
参考译文
汉译英翻译实务
原文
译文
学生译文（初稿、修改稿及终稿）
参考译文
翻译实务评析
词法层面
句法层面
语篇层面

第一节　背景知识与文本特点

一、人物简介翻译定义、分类及文本特点

人物简介是指通过简练的语言介绍个人信息。人物简介一般包括姓名、年龄、职业、成就等。人物简介的内容相对较少，国内外的学者多把焦点聚集在篇幅和内容都较长的传记上。中文将传记分为自传、他传、评传、回忆录等。其中“小传”主要介绍人物的主要生活经历和思想，而“简介”即简明扼要地介绍，是书面的简洁而全面地介绍。相较于“简介”，“小传”因其材料更加丰富翔实而篇幅更长。但是“简介”和“小传”中的事例都是从某个真实存在（过）的人物冗长繁杂的一生经历中选取出来的，因而它们所记叙的事件都是真实而有客观依据的，具有很强的说服力。所以，在“简介”和“小传”的原文本中多用陈述句和短句，以证明其所记载的内容的客观性和历史性。人物简介体现的是全面而简洁的人物信息，因而属于信息型文本。

二、人物简介翻译的原则与技巧

人物简介文本属于信息类文本，主要是陈述事实、信息等，用词比较严谨，多采用陈述句的表述。在对原文的相关词汇进行翻译时，译者需要考虑历史变迁因素，查阅相关历史资料，以确认词汇意义的正确性，选择与其概念意义对等的表达。由于人物简介英译的活动过程涉及不同的参与者，其中包括原文作者、译者和目的语读者。在翻译实践中，需要考虑到原语读者和目的语读者知识背景的差异性，对原文本进行深入分析，采用一定的翻译方法，以提供与人物介绍原文相对等的信息，实现原语信息共享，实现人际关系对等。在翻译时，原文和译文均采用陈述句的表达，在语气系统上保持陈述语气的一致性，可以实现人际意义对等。此外，译者在翻译过程中，应注意原文句子结构，并在译文中恰当使用衔接的表述，保持句子与句子之间的语意连贯，谋篇布局，实现语篇意义的对等。因此，在翻译人物简介文本时，应简单明了地传递与原文本相同的概念和信息。

第二节　专业术语与常用表达

ST	TT
1. 性别	gender
2. 籍贯	native place
3. 国籍	nationality
4. 民族	ethnicity
5. 出生年月	birth date
6. 现住址	current address
7. 婚姻状况	marital status
8. 家庭状况	family status
9. 健康状况	health status/condition
10. 教育背景	education background
11. 成就	accomplishment
12. 工作经历	work experience
13. 学士	bachelor
14. 硕士	master
15. 院士	academician
16. 其他技能和兴趣爱好	additional skills and interests
17. 先进工作者	advanced worker
18. 善于	be adept in
19. 被提升为	be promoted to
20. 打破纪录	break the record
21. 开发	exploit
22. 加快	expedite
23. 改进	improve
24. 被任命为	be nominated as
25. 突出贡献	outstanding contribution

续表

ST	TT
26.职业	occupation
27.独家采访	exclusive interview
28.负有不可推卸的责任	bear unshakeable responsibility
29.坚信	have the full conviction
30.连续报道	Folo(=follow -up)
31.民意调查	opinion poll
32.媒体炒作	media hype
33.年度风云人物	man of the year
34.深入采访	dig out in-depth interviews
35.抢先报道的独家新闻	scoop
36.硕果累累	yield fruitful results
37.特别提到	make a special mention
38.统筹兼顾	give overall consideration
39.专题报道	special reports
40.综合报道	round-up
41.按现状看来	as things stand
42.当之无愧的获奖者	deserved winners
43.长篇采访	feature-length interview
44.从长远讲	for the long haul
45.时间段	time slot
46.维护价值观	uphold one's values
47.有保留地,持怀疑态度地	with a grain of salt
48.高度重视	put a premium on
49.全局观念	overarching concept
50.提出忧虑	raise concerns about

第三节　英译汉翻译实务

一、原文

Born on 28 November 1902 in St John's, Newfoundland, Elizabeth Vera Crosbie Perlin is known for her pioneering work in providing education for children with special needs and developmental challenges.

During her lifetime she received several awards, including first person to be named St John's Citizen of the Year in 1962, Newfoundland Woman of the Century from the National Jewish Council in 1967, Officer of the Order of Canada in 1968, and an Honorary Doctorate of Law from Memorial University in 1970.

Vera Perlin received her education in St John's and Toronto. In 1926 she married Albert B. Perlin; they had three children, Ann Elizabeth, John and George.

She helped to establish Newfoundland's first Home and School Association and served on the advisory board of the United Church Orphanage.

It was during her tenure on this board that she became aware of the lack of educational facilities for developmentally challenged children.

二、学生译文初稿

伊丽莎白·维拉·克罗斯比·佩林于1902年11月28日出生于纽芬兰的圣约翰，因其在为有特殊需要和发展挑战的儿童提供教育方面的开拓性工作而闻名。

在她的一生中，她获得了多个奖项，包括1962年被提名为“圣约翰年度公民”的第一人，1967年国家犹太理事会颁发的“纽芬兰世纪女性”奖，1968年加拿大勋章和荣誉奖和1970年获得纪念大学法学博士学位。

维拉·柏林在圣约翰和多伦多接受了教育。1926年，她与阿尔伯特·珀林结婚；他们有三个孩子，安妮·伊丽莎白，约翰和乔治。

她帮助建立了纽芬兰的第一个家庭和学校协会，并在联合教会孤儿院的咨询委员会任职。

在任职董事会期间，她意识到缺乏针对发育障碍儿童所建立的教育设施。

——译员：张云燕

三、学生译文修改稿

ST1: Born on 28 November 1902 in St John's, Newfoundland, Elizabeth Vera Crosbie Perlin is known for her pioneering work in providing education for children with special needs and developmental challenges.

TT1：伊丽莎白·克洛斯比·维拉·珀林于1902年11月28日出生于纽芬兰的圣约翰，因其在为有特殊需要和遭遇发育障碍的儿童提供教育方面所做的开创性贡献而闻名。

删除[乔]：伊丽莎白·维拉·克罗斯比·佩林

删除[乔]：发展挑战

删除[乔]：的开拓性工作

ST2: During her lifetime she received several awards, including first person to be named St John's Citizen of the Year in 1962, Newfoundland Woman of the Century from the National Jewish Council in 1967, Officer of the Order of Canada in 1968, and an Honorary Doctorate of Law from Memorial University in 1970.

TT2：她一生中曾获得过多个奖项，其中包括1962年被提名为"圣约翰年度公民"，她是获此殊荣的第一人，1967年国家犹太委员会授予"纽芬兰世纪女性"奖，1968年在加拿大被授予勋章，1970年被纪念大学授予法学荣誉博士学位。

删除[乔]：在她的一生中，她获得了多个奖项

删除[2]：授予

删除[乔]：理事会

删除[乔]：颁发的

删除[乔]：和荣誉奖和

删除[乔]：获得

ST3: Vera Perlin received her education in St John's and Toronto. In 1926 she married Albert B. Perlin; they had three children, Ann Elizabeth, John and George.

TT3：维拉·珀林在圣约翰和多伦多接受了教育。1926

删除[乔]：柏林

年，她与阿尔伯特·珀林结婚；婚后他们育有三个孩子，分别是安妮·伊丽莎白，约翰和乔治。

删除[乔]: 他们有

ST4: She helped to establish Newfoundland's first Home and School Association and served on the advisory board of the United Church Orphanage.

TT4: 她帮助成立了纽芬兰地区第一个家庭学校协作会，并担任了教会孤儿联合会的顾问。

删除[乔]: 建立了

删除[乔]: 的

删除[乔]: 家庭和学校协会

删除[乔]: 并在联合教会孤儿院的咨询委员会任职

ST5: It was during her tenure on this board that she became aware of the lack of educational facilities for developmentally challenged children.

TT5: 也正是在这个委员会任职期间，她了解到发育障碍儿童教育设施的短缺。

删除[乔]: 在任职董事会期间

删除[乔]: 她意识到缺乏针对发育障碍儿童所建立的教育设施

审校员：乔婷
审校时间：2020.4.11

四、学生译文终稿

伊丽莎白·克洛斯比·维拉·珀林于1902年11月28日出生于纽芬兰的圣约翰，因其在为有特殊需要和遭遇发育障碍的儿童提供教育方面所做的开创性贡献而闻名。

她一生中曾获得过多个奖项，其中包括1962年被提名为“圣约翰年度公民”，她是获此殊荣的第一人，1967年国家犹太委员会授予 “纽芬兰世纪女性”奖，1968年在加拿大被授予勋章，1970年被纪念大学授予法学荣誉博士学位。

维拉·珀林在圣约翰和多伦多接受了教育。1926年，她与阿尔伯特·珀林结婚；婚后他们育有三个孩子，分别是安妮·伊丽莎白，约翰和乔治。

她帮助成立了纽芬兰地区第一个家庭学校协作会，并担任了教会孤儿联合会的顾问。

也正是在这个委员会任职期间，她了解到发育障碍儿童教育设施的短缺。

审校员：乔婷
审校时间：2020.4.11

五、参考译文

伊丽莎白・维拉・克罗斯比・珀林1902年11月28日出生于加拿大纽芬兰省圣・约翰斯市。她因为特殊需要和遭遇发育障碍的儿童提供教育方面做出开创性贡献而闻名。

她一生曾获得多个奖项：1962年被授予“圣•约翰斯年度公民”，她是获得此项殊荣的第一人；1967年被全国犹太人委员会授予“纽芬兰世纪妇女”称号；1968年被授予“加拿大功勋官员”；1970年被纪念大学授予法学名誉博士学位。

维拉・珀林曾在圣・约翰斯和多伦多接受教育。1926年与艾伯特・珀林结婚，育有三个子女：安・伊丽莎白、约翰和乔治。

她帮助纽芬兰成立了第一个“家庭学校联合会”，并在“联合基督教会孤儿院”顾问委员会任职。

也正是在这个委员会任职期间，她意识到发育障碍儿童教育设备的短缺。

第四节　汉译英翻译实务

一、原文

朱自清（1898—1948），字佩弦，浙江绍兴人，是我国著名的文学家、清华大学教授。

他一生清贫。1948年，由于国民党统治区政治腐败，物价飞涨，朱自清身为清华大学中文系主任，每月薪水也只能买三袋面粉，一家人时常缺吃少穿。

他本人身体十分虚弱，胃病日益严重，却无钱医治。

二、学生译文初稿

Zhu Ziqing（1898-1948), with another name - Pei Xian, from Shaoxing, Zhejiang, is a famous writer in China and a professor at Tsinghua University.

He lived in poverty all his life.In 1948, due to political corruption and soaring prices in the Kuomintang ruled area, Zhu Ziqing, the head of the Chinese Department of Tsinghua University, can only buy three bags of flour per month on his salary. His family was often short of food and clothing.

He is very weak, and his stomach is getting worse, but he has no money to cure it.

——译员：张云燕

三、学生译文修改稿

ST1: 朱自清（1898—1948），字佩弦，浙江绍兴人，是我国著名的文学家、清华大学教授。

TT1: Zhu Ziqing (1898-1948), courtesy-named Pei Xian, is a native of Shaoxing country, Zhejiang province. He was a famous writer in China and professor of Tsinghua University.

删除[乔]: with another name –

删除[乔]: from Shaoxing, Zhejiang,

删除[乔]: is

删除[乔]: a

删除[乔]: at

ST2: 他一生清贫。1948 年，由于国民党统治区政治腐败，物价飞涨，朱自清身为清华大学中文系主任，每月薪水也只能买三袋面粉，一家人时常缺吃少穿。

TT2: Zhu Ziqing was poor but remained clean all through his life. In 1948 when the prices rampantly soared under the corruptive rule by Kuomintang government Zhu Ziqing, the head of the Department of Chinese Language and Literature of Tsinghua University, can only earned a salary that was the equivalent of three bags of flour per month. As a result his family often suffered the scarcities of basic necessities.

删除[乔]: He lived in poverty

删除[乔]: , due to political corruption and soaring prices in the Kuomintang ruled area,

删除[乔]: Chinese

删除[乔]: buy

删除[乔]: on his salary

ST3: 他本人身体十分虚弱，胃病日益严重，却无钱医治。

TT3: In spite of his delicate health and even worsening stomach trouble, he could not afford to go to hospital.

删除[乔]: He is very weak, and his stomach is getting worse

审校员:乔婷

审校时间：2020.4.11

四、学生译文终稿

Zhu Ziqing（1898 - 1948), courtesy name Peixian, was born in Shaoxing, Zhejiang province. He was a renowned literateur and a professor of Tsinghua University.

He was poor but remained clean through his lifetime. In 1948, due to the corruptive politics and soaring prices caused by the administration of Kuomintang, Zhu Ziqing, dean of the Chinese language and literature department, could only afford no more than three sacks of flour a month on his salary. His family often suffered sacrifices of food and clothing.

He was in poor health and bore the deteriorating stomach trouble, but got no necessary treatment for financial reasons.

审校员：乔婷

审校时间：2020.04.11

五、参考译文

Zhu Ziqing（1898–1948), courtesy name Peixian, is native of Shaoxing county, Zhejiang province. He was a famous writer and professor of Tsinghua University.

Zhu Ziqing was poor but remained clean all his life. In 1948 when corruptive politics and soaring prices were rampant in Kuo Min Tang controlled area, Zhu Ziqing, Dean of the Department of Chinese Language and Literature, earned a salary that was enough only to buy three sacks of flour, and his family always suffered the scarcities of basic necessities.

In spite of his delicate health and worsening stomach trouble, he could not afford to go to the hospital.

第五节　翻译实务评析

一、词法分析

人物简介是较为特殊的信息型文本，内容以传递事实信息为主，因而要求译文准确如实地传达原文内容。译者在翻译人物简介时应做到语言简练、选词恰当、表述得体。例如，原文（汉译英）中，“only”在中文翻译中包含有“仅有的，唯一的，最好的，最恰当的”等多种含义。基于对朱自清的简朴生平介绍，译文采用了最为合理的“only”一词。其次，译者应根据特定语境做出恰当的词性转换。例如，原文（汉译英）中“他一生清贫”一句的“清贫”指“生活清寒贫苦”，为形容词词性，在学生译文初稿中，将其进行词性转换，译为“lived in poverty”，转换为名词词性，使译文更加符合译入语习惯，更为忠实明了地传达原语文本的思想内容。但在学生译文终稿及参考译文中，将其译为“He was poor but remained clean through his lifetime”，过度解读原文内容，未能体现人物简介文本真实性的特征。

二、句法分析

人物简介文本多采用陈述句的表述，在文本中多使用简单句。例如："It was during her tenure on this board that she became aware of the lack of educational facilities for developmentally challenged children"中，原文采用了强调句式来突出伊丽莎白·克洛斯比·维拉·珀林做出的贡献，译者采取了直译法，遵循原文的语体特征和行文风格，也便于中文读者更好的了解到她的生平贡献。在汉译英第二段中，首句是短句，第二句是一个长句，译者在翻译过程中，对原句结构进行了重新划分，采用拆译的方法将第二句单独进行翻译使译文行文更加顺畅。

三、语篇分析

人物简介体现的是全面而简洁的人物信息，用词严谨，结构紧密，要求译者在翻译实践中注重原文的完整性与同一性。例如：原文（汉译英）"他本人身体十分虚弱，胃病日益严重，却无钱医治。"一句中出现了"却"一词，表示与上文的衔接转折的文字，在英译时，补充介词短语"in spite of"表达其逻辑关系，体现了中英文形合意合的差异，也有益于目的语读者对原文信息的接受与理解。

【课外拓展】

你校邀请国外知名学家进行演讲，与会人员有来自不同国家的语言学及翻译学教授，请你拟好与会人员的名单，并使用英语介绍各位来宾。

文献参考

[1]蔡力坚．什么是忠实性[J]．中国翻译,2020(01):185—187.

[2]曹心羽．翻译补偿在人物传记中的运用[D]．上海交通大学,2018.

[3]冯庆华．实用翻译教程[M]．上海:上海外语教育出版社,2010.

[4]黄忠廉．翻译项目管理[M]．北京:国防工业出版社,2014.

[5]李长栓．非文学翻译[M]．北京:外语教学与研究出版社,2004.

[6]王克非．翻译文化史论[M]．上海:上海外语教育出版社,1997.

[7]杨正润．传记文学史纲[M]．南京:江苏教育出版社,1994.

[8]叶子南．散谈传记翻译[J]．中国翻译,2005(05):91-92.

[9]叶子南．谈传记文本的翻译[J]．中国翻译,2007(03):82-84.

[10]张坤．传记文学的翻译策略[J]．安徽文学,2015(02):30-31.

[11]赵白生．传记文学理论[M]．北京:北京大学出版社,2003.

第十一章 演讲辞翻译

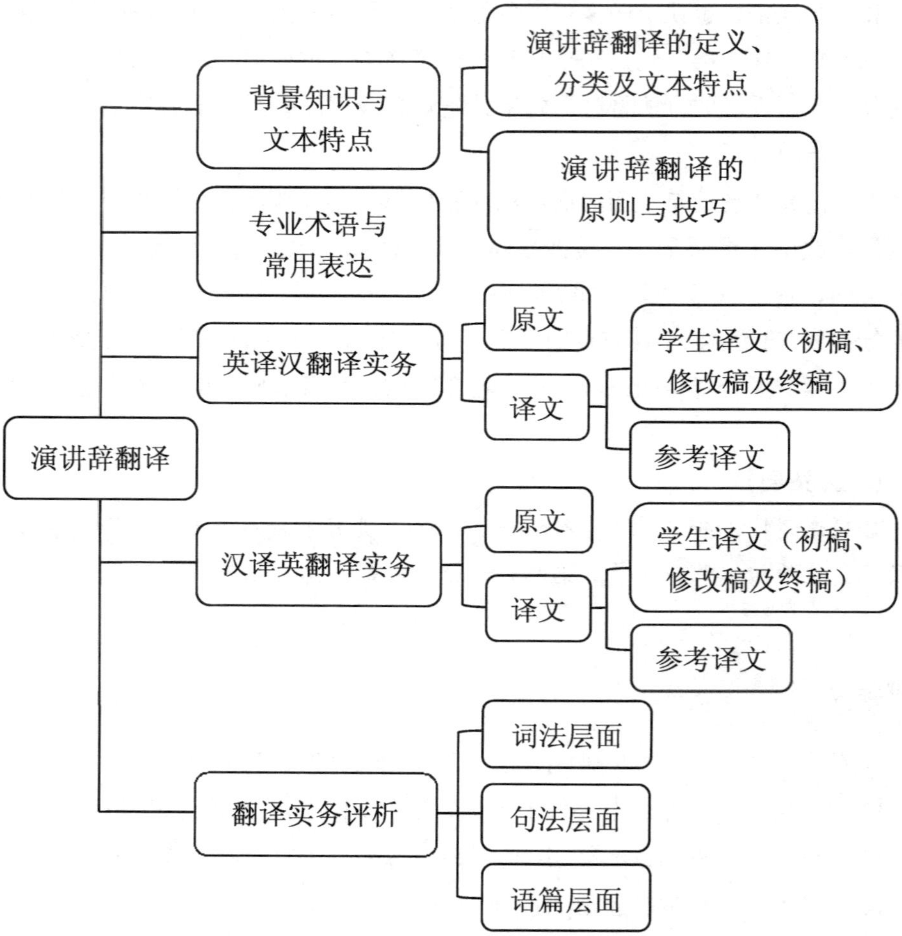
演讲辞翻译
背景知识与文本特点
演讲辞翻译的定义、分类及文本特点
演讲辞翻译的原则与技巧
专业术语与常用表达
英译汉翻译实务
原文
译文
学生译文（初稿、修改稿及终稿）
参考译文
汉译英翻译实务
原文
译文
学生译文（初稿、修改稿及终稿）
参考译文
翻译实务评析
词法层面
句法层面
语篇层面

第一节　背景知识与文本特点

一、演讲辞翻译定义、分类及文本特点

演讲辞的目的在于表达讲话人的情感，发表自己的主张，从而引起号召作用。通过演讲，讲话人可以把自己的思想感情传达给听众，旨在产生一定的作用和影响，达到宣传的作用。从演讲内容划分，主要有政治演讲、生活演讲、法律演讲等；从演讲方式划分，有叙述式演讲、议论式演讲、抒情式演讲等；从演讲情调划分，有激昂型演讲、深沉型演讲、严谨型演讲等；从演讲形式划分，有命题演讲、即兴演讲和论辩演讲等；从演讲目的划分，有说服性演讲、鼓动性演讲、传授性演讲等。演讲辞类文本特征特点鲜明，从语法、修辞等方面可总结出以下三个语言特点：

1.规范口语。规范的口语是指语言容易理解，句子符合句法、语法；

2.结合长短句。一般而言，长句指的是用词多、结构复杂的句子；短句则是用词少、结构简单的句子；

3.运用修辞。长句与短句巧妙结合使用，短句短小，简洁，从而听起来有种抑扬顿挫的韵律。

二、演讲辞翻译的原则与技巧

演讲内容旨在传播思想，给人们精神启发，它的语言通俗、简洁、并且有一种振奋人心的号召力。因此演讲文本翻译时应遵循以下三个原则：（一）精确性原则。准确性指原文的内容和形式，包括原文修辞与风格的精确传递；（二）连贯性原则。演讲的目的在于短时间内激发听众、感染听众，它的语言逻辑性强，句子和段落的内在联系密切，因为只有这样才能吸引听众的注意力；(三)恰当性原则。恰当性原则是指在翻译演讲文本中应该考虑到演讲的内容和背景，要使译文语言恰当、不偏离，不出错。“恰当性”在翻译实践中尤为重要，恰当的译文在词汇、句式、风格上适合具体文体的需要。

第二节 专业术语与常用表达

ST	TT
1.非常荣幸	it's an honor
2.首先	to begin with
3.两部分组成	consist of two parts
4.简要总结	brief summary
5.在我结束之前	before I finish
6.结束我的演讲	to close my speech
7.总结	to sum up
8.正如你所见	as you can see
9.总而言之	in conclusion
10.那就这样	that's all
11.感谢您的参加	thank you for your attention
12.感谢您的聆听	thank you for your listening
13.就这些	so much for
14.这就是…的结尾	That's the end of
15.我不得不在这里停止	I have to stop here
16.这有一些	there are some
17.最好的那一个	the best one
18.以下的评论	with the following comments
19.通过列出所有的因素	by listing out all the factors
20.指出	point out
21.以下方面	the following aspects
22.以下总结	the following conclusion
23.让我们一起看一下	let's look at
24.我所讲的内容	what I have talked about
25.…的结尾	the end of
26.我的陈述	my presentation

续表

ST	TT
27.一个简短的总结	a brief summary
28.我想说的是	let me just say
29.我会给大家展示	I'll show you
30.极大的荣幸	it is a great privilege
31.汇总表	summary statement
32.重点	major points
33.首先讲讲	first talk about
34.然后谈论	then touch on
35.最后讨论	and finally discuss
36.以下标题	under the following headings
37.第一部分解决	the first part deals with
38.第二部分解决	the second part concerns
39.女士们,先生们,有机会给各位尊贵的听众演讲,我感到非常荣幸。	Ladies and gentlemen, it's an honor to have the opportunity to address such a distinguished audience
40.我很荣幸在这个极其重要的时刻发表演讲。	It is a great privilege to have this opportunity to say a few words on this extremely important occasion of …
41.让我们从这项新技术的理论基础开始。	Let us start with the theoretical basis of this new technique.
42.我们必须率先考虑这个原则。	To begin with, we have to consider the principle.
43.我的演讲分为四个部分。	I've divided my presentation into four parts.
44.我今天的演讲包括两个部分,一个是……另一个是……	My talk today consists of two parts. One is... and the other is...
45.在结束我的演讲之前,我将向你们展示最后一张幻灯片。	To close my speech, I'll show you the last slide
46.让我们一起回顾我的演说内容。	Let's look at what I have talked about.
47.现在我想做个总结。	Now I'd like to summarize my talk.
48.让我用以下几点概述我的发言。	Let me conclude my talk with the following comments.
49.我的演讲到此结束。	That's the end of my presentation.
50.如你所知,有一些强有力的理由……	As you can see, there are some very good reasons ...

第三节 英译汉翻译实务

一、原文

The year 2020 also marks the fifth anniversary of China-UK "Golden Era" launched by President Xi Jinping's state visit to the UK in 2015. A few days ago, President Xi and Prime Minister Johnson had a telephone conversation. This conversation charted the course for the development of China-UK relations.

China and the UK are natural partners in building a community with a shared future for mankind. Both are permanent members of the UN Security Council. Both champion multilateralism and support free trade. And both are great civilizations and regard as their mission to promote world peace and development. It is important that the two countries take up more responsibilities and make more efforts in building a community with a shared future for mankind.

First, China and the UK should build up consensus, especially on safeguarding multilateralism and free trade, opposing unilateralism and protectionism, and promoting win-win cooperation. It is important that our two countries accommodate each others' core interests and major concerns on the basis of mutual respect. In doing so, the two countries will be able to form a new type of state-to-state relations and will set an example for relationship between major Eastern and Western countries.

二、学生译文初稿

2020年也标志着习近平主席于2015年对英国进行国事访问而启动的中英"黄金时代"五周年。几天前，习主席与约翰逊总理进行了电话交谈。这次对话描绘了中英关系发展的历程。

中国和英国是建立人类共同未来社区的自然伙伴。他们都是联合国安理会常任理事国。双方都拥护多边主义并支持自由贸易。两者都是伟大的文明，都视促进世界和平与发展为使命。两国承担着更多责任，最重要的是为建立人类共同未来的社区作出更多努力。

首先，中英应该建立共识，特别是在维护多边主义和自由贸易，反对单边主义和贸易保护主义，促进双赢合作方面。我们两国必须在相互尊重的基础上容纳彼此的核心利益和重大关切，这点很重要。这样，两国将能够建立一种新型的国与国之间的关系，并将为东西部主要国家之间的关系树立榜样。

——译员：王鹏燕

三、学生译文修改稿

2020 年也是习近平主席于 2015 年对英国进行国事访问发起的中英"黄金时代"五周年。几天前，习近平主席与约翰逊首相进行了电话会谈。这为中英关系的发展指明了方向。

中英两国是构建人类命运共同体的自然伙伴，两国都是联合国安理会常任理事国。双方自觉拥护多边主义，并支持发展自由贸易。两国都具有悠久的文明，都以促进世界和平与发展为己任。两国积极承担责任，最重要的是为建立人类命运共同体作出更多的努力。

一是凝聚共识，着重在维护多边主义和自由贸易方面、反对单边主义和贸易保护主义、以促进合作共赢。两国必须在相互尊重的基础上协调好两国的核心利益和重大事务。这样做，两国将能够建立新型国与国之间的关系，并将为东西方主要国家之间良好关系的建立树立榜样。

删除[乔]: 标志着

删除[乔]: 这次对话会谈主要描绘了中英关系发展的历程

删除[乔]: 建立

删除[A]: 最好搭档

删除[乔]: 属

删除[乔]: 史

删除[乔]: 的使命

删除[乔]: 首先，中英应该

删除[乔]: 建立共识

删除[乔]: ，这一点很重要

审校员：乔婷

审校时间：2020. 03. 21

四、学生译文终稿

2020年也是习近平主席于2015年对英国进行国事访问开启中英"黄金时代"五周年。几天前，习近平主席与约翰逊首相进行了电话会晤，这为中英关系发展指明了方向。

中国和英国是构建人类命运共同体的天然伙伴。两国都是联合国安理会常任理事国。双方自觉拥护多边主义，支持发展自由贸易。两者都有伟大的文明，都以促进世界和平与发展为己任。两国应肩负起更多责任，为构建人类命运共同体作出更多努力。一是凝聚共识，特别是在维护多边主义和自由贸易、反对单边主义和贸易保护主义、促进双赢合作等方面。我们两国应该在相互尊重的基础上维护彼此的核心利益和重大关切。这样，两国将形成新型国家关系，为东西方国家良好关系的建立树立榜样。

审校员：乔婷

审校时间：2020.3.21

五、参考译文

2020年也是习近平主席访英开启中英关系“黄金时代”五周年。不久前，习近平主席与约翰逊首相通电话，为两国关系发展指明了方向。

在构建人类命运共同体方面，中英是天然合作伙伴。两国同为联合国安理会常任理事国，都倡导多边主义、支持自由贸易，都是东西方文明具有代表性的国家，都肩负着促进世界和平与发展的重要使命。双方应在构建人类命运共同体上承担更多责任，展现更多作为。

一是凝聚理念共识。双方应坚定维护多边主义和自由贸易，反对单边主义和保护主义，坚持互利共赢合作导向，在相互尊重基础上照顾彼此核心利益和重大关切，树立新型国际关系和东西方大国交往的典范。

第四节　汉译英翻译实务

一、原文

严格彻底的防控措施正在显现效果。截至2月14日，全国除湖北以外的确诊病例已经连续12天下降，而湖北和武汉的疫情也正在得到更有效管控。这一事实表明，这场疫情总体上是可控的。治愈人数昨天超过了8000人，全国病亡率控制在2.29%，除湖北以外的病亡率则为0.55%。这一事实和数据表明，这场疫情总体上是可治的。正像习近平主席所说，我们完全有信心、有能力、有把握战胜这场疫情。黎明，正在到来；曙光，就在前方。

疫情确实给中国的经济和社会发展带来了挑战，但这将是阶段性、暂时性的。中国经济有着强劲韧性、巨大潜力和丰沛活力，我们完全有条件抵御各种风险挑战，中国经济大势长期向好的基本面没有也不会改变。

二、学生译文初稿

The prevention and control measures we have been taking are having an impact. As of 14 February, the number of confirmed cases nationwide, except in Hubei, had a continuous decline for 12 days, and the outbreaks in Hubei and Wuhan were being more effectively controlled. This indicates that the epidemic is generally manageable. More than

8,000 people recovered yesterday, and the nationwide fatality rate was controlled at 2.29% and 0.55% except in Hubei, which suggests that the epidemic is generally treatable. As President Xi Jinping had said, we are fully confident that we have the ability to overcome this epidemic. The dawn of victory is coming .

The epidemic has indeed brought challenges to China's economic and social development, but this will be periodic and temporary. The Chinese economy is strong, resilient, promising and dynamic. we are able to withstand all kinds of risks and challenges. China's long-term economic fundamentals have not been changed and will be not changed.

——译员：牛婷

三、学生译文修改稿

The strict and thorough prevention and control measures adopted by Chinese government are showing results. As of February 14, the number of confirmed cases, except in Hubei, had a continuous decline for 12 days, and the outbreaks in Hubei and Wuhan were being more effectively controlled. It indicates that the epidemic is generally manageable. More than 8,000 people were cured yesterday, and the nationwide fatality rate was controlled at 2.29% and 0.55% except in Hubei, which suggests that the epidemic is generally curable. As President Xi Jinping said, we are fully confident that we have the ability to overcome this epidemic. The dawn of victory is coming. The epidemic has indeed brought challenges to China's economic and social development, but this will be periodic and temporary. Due to its strong resilience, great potential and vitality, the Chinese economy can overcome all risks and challenges. The long-term fundamentals of the Chinese economy have not changed and will not change.

审校：张静&杨雯
日期：2020.03.21

删除[杨]: we have been taking are having an impact

删除[杨]: 14

删除[杨]: nationwide

删除[杨]: This

删除[杨]: recovered

删除[杨]: controoled

删除[杨]: treatable

删除[杨]: The Chinese economy is strong, resilient, promising and dynamic. we are able to withstand all kinds of risks and challenges.

删除[杨]: China's long-term economic fundamentals have not been changed and will be not changed.

四、学生译文终稿

The strict and thorough prevention and control measures adopted by Chinese government are showing results. As of February 14, the number of confirmed cases, except in Hubei, had a continuous decline for 12 days, and the outbreaks in Hubei and Wuhan were being more effectively controlled. It indicates that the epidemic is generally manageable. More than 8,000 people were cured yesterday, and the nationwide fatality rate was controlled at 2.29% and 0.55% except in Hubei, which suggests that the epidemic is generally curable. As President Xi Jinping said, we are fully confident that we have the ability to overcome this epidemic. The dawn of victory is coming.

The epidemic has indeed brought challenges to China's economic and social development, but this will be periodic and temporary. Due to its strong resilience, great potential and vitality, the Chinese economy can overcome all risks and challenges. The long-term fundamentals of the Chinese economy have not changed and will not change.

审校员：张静&杨雯

审校时间：2020.03.21

五、参考译文

China's rigorous and thorough measures are paying off. As of 14th. February, the number of confirmed cases outside Hubei has recorded a 12-day consecutive drop, and the situation in Hubei and Wuhan is being put under more effective containment. This shows that overall, the epidemic is controllable. The number of cured cases exceeded 8, 000 as of yesterday. The case fatality rate has been kept at around 2.29 percent nationwide, and 0.55 percent outside Hubei. These facts and figures demonstrate that the disease is largely curable. Just as President Xi Jinping said, we have full confidence, capacity and determination to defeat the epidemic. Dawn is breaking and we are seeing light coming through.

The challenges the outbreak has posed to China's economic and social development will be temporary and short-lived. With its strong resilience, potential and vitality, the Chinese economy is well positioned to overcome all risks and challenges. The fundamentals sustaining sound economic growth have not changed and will not change.

第五节　翻译实务评析

一、词法分析

演讲是一种面向公众的活动，在演讲辞中常常包含大量精确信息的传递，如数字、头衔、部门名称、专有名词等。其中，数字翻译要求译者在掌握中英文间数字翻译的技巧与方法的基础上做到精准无误。对于较小的数字可以采用目的语中相应的数字单位进行直接翻译，而面对较大的数字时，译者需考虑中英文中数字表达习惯，进行适当的单位换算，确保原文中的数字在译文中清晰呈现。例如：译者将原文（汉译英）中“超过了8000”“2.29%”“0.55%”等各个含有数字表达的部分在译文中都做了适当的转换，确保了信息传达的真实性与准确性。此外，演讲辞中多见不同领域的专业术语。例如：原文（英译汉）中出现的“multilateralism”“unilateralism”和“protectionism”等词，均属于经济领域的专业术语，译者通过查询资料及相关参考文献后采取直译法将其呈现在译文中，使得译文更加权威可信。

二、句法分析

英语是一门重视句式结构的语言，而汉语句式结构较为松散。例如：原文（英译汉）中包含大量主语从句，旨在避免因主语过长而导致句子头重脚轻。但这种长句表达在汉语中比较少见，所以译者在翻译时根据汉语表达习惯将原句拆分为多个短句，使译文中的句意表达与原文达到等同的效果。汉语习惯使用对仗句或排比句来突出情感的强烈，英语更加看重句意的传递，但为了使译文结构忠实于原文，有时译者也需参照原文对译文进行类似处理。例如：原文（汉译英）中“黎明，正在到来；曙光，就在前方”，译者在翻译时只将“黎明即将到来”的这一句核心意思呈现出来，但参考译文将原句的前后两部分以连接词“and”衔接，这样不仅没有削弱原文的情感表达力度，也在结构上尽量贴近原文句式。

三、语篇分析

演讲辞论点鲜明，逻辑紧密，整篇文章的谋篇布局都以核心观点为准，这就决定了演讲辞具有不同于其它文本的语篇特点。所以，代词、表示逻辑的连词等在演讲辞中都更为常见。例如：原文（英译汉）中“both”“and”以及“first”等词使用较多，在翻译时，鉴于演讲辞语篇的独特性，译者绝不可打破这种原有的逻辑关系，要将其在译文中完整无缺地体现出来。中英文演讲辞中，句与句、段与段间都存在着显性或隐性的逻辑关系，所以无论是进行英译汉还是汉译英，译者都应考虑到演讲辞的这种语篇特点，切不可忽略文章本身的关联性及上下文的衔接性。在译文中，译者借用“这”“都”及“首先”等词精炼鲜明地体现了原文的逻辑关系。

【课外拓展】

一年一度的文化节又开幕了，请你与团队模拟情境，对文化节开幕式领导致辞进行翻译。

文献参考

[1]陈蕾蕾．英语演讲中隐喻的汉译[D]．湖南师范大学,2013．

[2]郭文静．目的论视角下政务演讲中对中国特色词汇的翻译研究[J]．课程教育研究,2016(37):9．

[3]方梦之．应用翻译研究:原理、策略与技巧[M]．上海:上海外语教育出版社,2013．

[4]黄忠廉．翻译项目管理[M]．北京:国防工业出版社,2014．

[5]李国华．词源学视角下的奥巴马演讲辞翻译策略研究[J]．上海翻译,2013(04):28-31．

[6]谭梦．关于演讲词翻译的探讨[J]．湖南第一师范学院学报,2015,15(03):95-99．

[7]王军平．演讲翻译的尺度[J]．中国科技翻译,2009,22(04):33-37．

[8]余樟亚．英语政治演讲的翻译策略[J]．中国科技翻译,2019,32(04):52-54．

[9]杨明星．外交语境中“中国梦”核心话语英译辨析[J]．中国翻译,2016,37(06):86-91．

[10]杨明星,齐静静．外交修辞的复合性翻译标准:“政治等效+审美再现”——以国家领导外交演讲古诗文为例[J]．中国外语,2018,15(06):89-96+109．

[11]周红,朱芙蓉．政治演讲中隐喻的翻译[J]．湖南人文科技学院学报,2010(01):85-87．

[12]张志慧．奥巴马获胜演讲中转喻的解读与翻译[J]．中国科技翻译,2009,22(02):52-55．

第十二章 旅游翻译

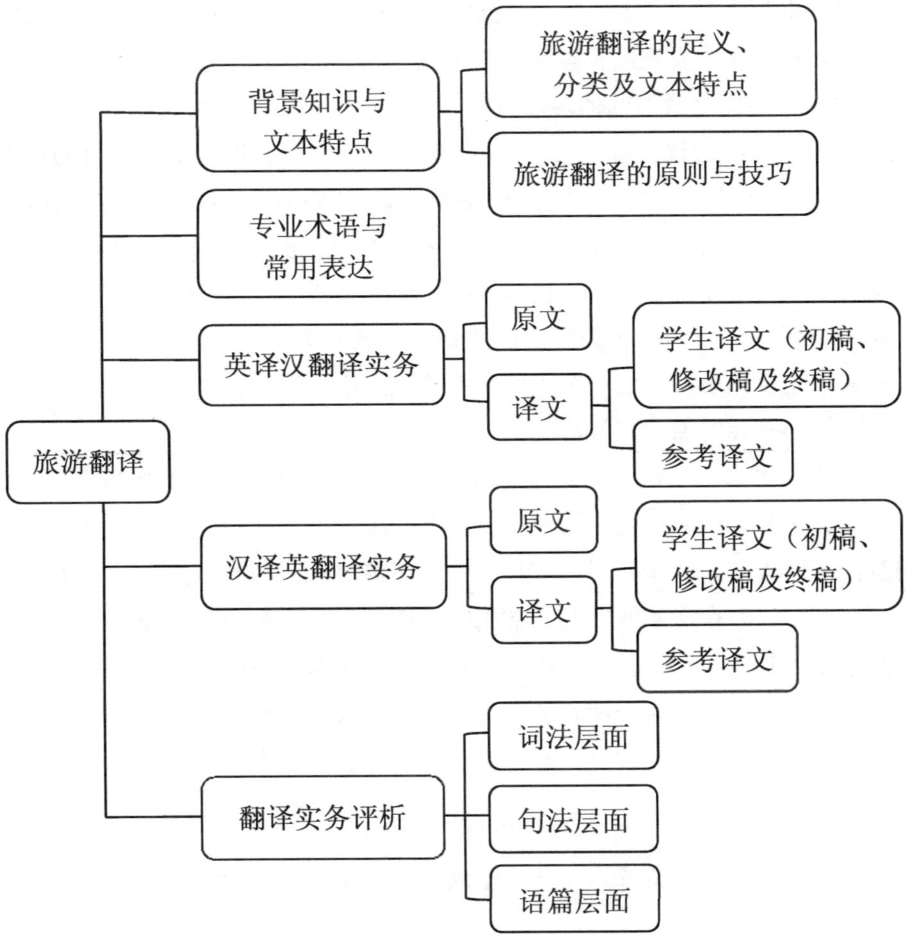
旅游翻译
背景知识与文本特点
旅游翻译的定义、分类及文本特点
旅游翻译的原则与技巧
专业术语与常用表达
英译汉翻译实务
原文
译文
学生译文（初稿、修改稿及终稿）
参考译文
汉译英翻译实务
原文
译文
学生译文（初稿、修改稿及终稿）
参考译文
翻译实务评析
词法层面
句法层面
语篇层面

第一节　背景知识与文本特点

一、旅游翻译定义、分类及文本特点

中国是世界上对“旅游”具有最早文字记载的国家。“旅”和“游”二字是在山东昌乐骨刻文中发现的，也是东夷平民有关旅游娱乐活动最早的记录，同时它也是中国旅游文化最早的体现。“旅”是旅行、外出，即基于某一目的在空间上从甲地到乙地的行程过程；“游”是外出游览、观光，即为了实现目的所做的旅行，二者结合即为旅游。旅游翻译主要包括旅游指南、旅游行程、旅游委托书、旅游合同、旅游广告、旅游表格、旅游解说词、景点介绍、参观点介绍、博物馆说词、旅游推销手册、旅游宣传册、旅游地图、文艺演出节目单、餐厅菜单、宾馆指示牌、公园指示牌等方面的翻译。旅游类文本特征显著，特点鲜明，通俗易懂。主要具有文学性、艺术性、宣传性及广告性等特点。

二、旅游翻译的原则与技巧

翻译旅游文本，译者必须要考虑到文本的可读性及读者的接受效果。英译旅游宣传材料主要是以外国友人为对象，以此介绍并发展中国的旅游行业。旅游文本的翻译不同于其它文本翻译，其具有向游客传递、介绍景点信息和传递文化的功能。在翻译旅游类文本时，我们首先需要遵循旅游文本的功能和目的，忠实传达原文信息。其次在翻译时也要遵循旅游文本的文本类型，在译文中体现广告宣传的语气。除此之外，迎合读者的文化和审美诉求，灵活处理文化和美学信息在旅游文本的翻译中也至关重要，需要采取灵活的翻译策略。

第二节　专业术语与常用表达

ST	TT
1. 旅游指南	guidebook
2. 旅游计划	itinerary
3. 淡季	low season
4. 旺季	high season

续表

ST	TT
5.标准价	standard rate
6.套房	suite
7.家庭套房	family suite
8.登记	registration
9.定金	deposit
10.取消预订	cancellation
11.贵重品	valuables
12.行李员	porter
13.行李	luggage
14.托运行李	checked luggage
15.行李收据	baggage receipt
16.手推车	trolley
17.公文包	briefcase
18.旅行袋	travelling bag
19.小提箱	suitcase
20.国际航班	international flight
21 国内航班	domestic flight
22.航空业务	airline operation
23.停机坪	landing field
24.单人房	single room
25.双人房	double room
26.大床房	king size room
27.经济间	budget room
28.标准间	standard room
29.高级套房	superior suite
30.旅馆	inn

续表

ST	TT
31.招待所	hostel
32.汽车饭店	motel
33.廉价旅馆	budget hotel
34.五星级饭店	five-star hotel
35.县旅游局	county tourism administration
36.世界旅游日	world tourism day
37.旅费	travelling expense
38旅游业	travel industry
39.旅游周刊	tourist periodical
40.旅游局	tourist authority
41.游览	sightseeing
42.旅游小册子	tour brochure
43.旅游团目录	tour catalog
44.国家级历史文化名城	state-list famous historical and culture cities
45.旅游团陪同	tour escort
46.领队	tour leader
47.旅游路线	tour route
48.旅游协会	tourist association
49.出入境手续	customs formality
50.私人物品	personal belongings

第三节 英译汉翻译实务

一、原文

On 30th January 2020, the WHO Director General has declared the outbreak of novel coronavirus 2019- NCoV as a Public Health Emergency of International Concern

(PHEIC), based on the advice of the Emergency Committee under the International Health Regulations(2005). Following that determination, WHO did not recommend any travel or trade restrictions, based on the current information available.

Evidence on travel measures that significantly interfere with international traffic for more than 24 hours shows that such measures may have a public health rationale at the beginning of the containment phase of an outbreak, as they may allow affected countries to implement sustained response measures, and non-affected countries to gain time to initiate and implement effective preparedness measures. Such restrictions, however, need to be short in duration, proportionate to the public health risks, and be reconsidered regularly as the situation evolves.

Countries should be prepared for containment, including active surveillance, early detection, isolation and case management, contact tracing and prevention of onward spread of 2019-NCoV infection, and to share full data with WHO. In accordance with their obligations under the Article 43 of the International Health Regulations (2005), States Parties must inform WHO about additional health measures that significantly interfere with international traffic.

二、学生译文初稿

2020年1月30日，世界卫生组织总干事根据突发事件委员会《国际卫生条例(2005年)》提出的建议，宣布2019年新型冠状病毒暴发为国际关注的突发公共卫生事件(PHEIC)。世卫组织据现有资料作出这项决定之后，不提倡任何旅行或贸易限制活动。

据旅游措施,明显干扰国际流量超过24小时显示,这些措施可能会有公共卫生基本原理开始爆发的控制阶段,因为他们可能允许受影响国家实现持续的响应措施,和未受感染国家赢得时间来发起和实施有效的防范措施。但是，这种限制必须是短期的，要与公共卫生风险相称，并根据情况的演变定期加以重新考虑。

各国应做好遏制准备，包括积极监测、早期发现、隔离和病例管理、追踪接触者和预防2019-新冠病毒感染的进一步传播，并与世卫组织共享完整数据。根据《国际卫生条例》(2005年)第43条规定的义务，缔约国必须向世卫组织通报严重干扰国际交通的其他卫生措施。

——译员：陈春

三、学生译文修改稿

2020 年 1 月 30 日，世卫组织总干事根据《国际卫生条例》（2005 年）所设应急委员会的建议，宣布 2019-NCoV 新型冠状病毒的爆发为国际关注的突发公共卫生事件（PHEIC）。根据这一决定，世卫组织根据现有资料，不建议任何旅行或贸易限制。

24 小时以上严重干扰国际交通的旅行措施的证据表明，这些措施在疫情遏制阶段开始时可能有公共健康理由，因为他们可能允许受影响国家实现持续的响应措施,和未受感染国家赢得时间来发起和实施有效的防范措施。但是，这种限制必须是短期的，要与公共卫生风险相称，并根据情况的演变定期加以重新考虑。

各国应做好遏制准备，包括积极监测、早期发现、隔离和病例管理、追踪接触者和预防 2019-新冠病毒感染的进一步传播，并与世卫组织共享完整数据。根据《国际卫生条例》(2005 年)第 43 条规定的义务，缔约国必须向世卫组织通报严重干扰国际交通的其他卫生措施。

删除[W]: 2020 年 1 月 30 日，世界卫生组织总干事根据突发事件委员会《国际卫生条例(2005 年)》提出的建议，宣布 2019 年新型冠状病毒暴发为国际关注的突发公共卫生事件(PHEIC)。世卫组织据现有资料作出这项决定之后，不提倡任何旅行或贸易限制活动。

删除[W]: 据旅游措施,明显干扰国际流量超过 24 小时显示,这些措施可能会有公共卫生基本原理开始爆发的控制阶段

审校员：何丽霞

审校时间：2020.3.21

四、学生译文终稿

2020 年 1 月 30 日，世界卫生组织总干事根据突发事件委员会《国际卫生条例(2005 年)》提出的建议，宣布 2019 年新型冠状病毒暴发为国际关注的突发公共卫生事件(PHEIC)。世卫组织据现有资料作出这项决定之后，不提倡任何旅行或贸易限制活动。

据旅游措施,明显干扰国际流量超过 24 小时显示,这些措施可能会有公共卫生基本原理开始爆发的控制阶段,因为他们可能允许受影响国家实现持续的响应措施,和未受感染国家赢得时间来发起和实施有效的防范措施。但是，这种限制必须是短期的，要与公共卫生风险相称，并根据情况的演变定期加以重新考虑。

各国应做好遏制准备，包括积极监测、早期发现、隔离和病例管理、追踪接触者和预防2019-新冠病毒感染的进一步传播，并与世卫组织共享完整数据。根据《国际卫生条例》(2005年)第43条规定的义务，缔约国必须向世卫组织通报严重干扰国际交通的其他卫生措施。

审校员：何丽霞

审校时间：2020.3.21

五、参考译文

2020年1月30日，根据《国际卫生条例》（2005年）所设应急委员会的建议，世界卫生组织总干事宣布2019-NCoV新型冠状病毒的爆发为国际公共卫生紧急事件（PHEIC）。基于这一决定及现实状况，世界卫生组织不提倡任何旅行或贸易限制活动。

24小时以上严重干扰国际交通的旅行措施的证据表明，这些措施可能会有公共卫生基本原理开始爆发的控制阶段,因为他们可能允许受影响国家实现持续的响应措施,和未受感染国家赢得时间来发起和实施有效的防范措施。但是，这种限制必须是短期之内，与公共卫生风险相称，并随着情况的发展而定期予以重新考虑。

各国应做好遏制的准备，包括积极监测、早期发现、隔离和病例管理、接触者追踪和预防2019-NCoV感染的进一步蔓延，并与世界卫生组织分享全部数据。根据《国际卫生条例》(2005年)第43条规定的义务，缔约国必须向世界卫生组织通报严重干扰国际贩运的其他卫生措施。

第四节　汉译英翻译实务

一、原文

对于决定从湖北省武汉市遣返其国民的国家，为确保遣返人员的健康和福祉，需要考虑以下关键因素。考虑采取措施，提高国家备灾能力，防止遣返前、遣返期间和遣返后进一步扩散。

登机前应采取的措施：

·出发前与主管部门加强双边沟通、协调和规划。

·飞机应配备足够的医务人员，以容纳预期人数的国民人数，并配备适当的

PPE和设备/用品，以应对途中的疾病。

·飞机的非医疗机组人员应得到适当的简报和装备，并注意体征和症状，以检测NCoV的有症状的乘客。

·出境筛查，例如温度测量和调查问卷，应在出发前进行，以便及早发现症状。筛查结果应与接受国共享。

·建议推迟通过出境检查发现疑似患病旅客的旅行，以便转介做进一步评估和治疗。

二、学生译文初稿

For countries that decide to repatriate their nationals from Wuhan, Hubei Province, the following key factors need to be considered to ensure the health and well-being of repatriates. In addition, measures to enhance national preparedness and prevent further proliferation before, during and after repatriation need to be considered.

Steps to Take before boarding:

·Strengthen bilateral communication, coordination and planning with competent authorities before departure.

·The aircraft should be adequately staffed with medical personnel to accommodate the anticipated number of nationals and equipped with appropriate PPE and equipment/supplies to respond to in-flight diseases.

·The non-medical crew of the aircraft should be properly briefed and equipped and pay attention to signs and symptoms to detect symptomatic passengers of the NCoV.

·Exit screening, such as temperature measurements and questionnaires, should be carried out before departure in order to detect symptoms early. Screening results should be Shared with recipient countries.

·It is recommended that travel of suspected sick passengers detected through exit screening be delayed for further assessment and treatment.

——译员：王婷婷

三、学生译文修改稿

For countries that decide to repatriate their nationals from Wuhan, Hubei Province, the following key factors need to be considered to ensure the health and well-being of repatriates. In addition, measures to enhance national preparedness and prevent further proliferation before, during and after repatriation need to be considered.

Measures to be adopted before embarkation

Strengthen bilateral communication, coordination and planning with competent authorities before departure.

删除[W]: Steps to Take before boarding:

The aircraft should be adequately staffed with medical personnel to accommodate the anticipated number of nationals and equipped with appropriate PPE and equipment/supplies to respond to in-flight diseases.

The non-medical crew of the aircraft should be properly briefed and equipped and pay attention to signs and symptoms to detect symptomatic passengers of the NCoV.

Exit screening, such as temperature measurements and questionnaires, should be carried out before departure in order to detect symptoms early. Screening results should be Shared with recipient countries.

It is recommended that travel of suspected sick passengers detected through exit screening be delayed for further assessment and treatment.

审校员：何丽霞

审校时间：2020.3.21

四、学生译文终稿

For countries that decide to repatriate their nationals from Hubei, Wuhan Province, the following key factors need to be considered to ensure the health and well–being of repatriates. In addition, measures to enhance national preparedness and prevent further proliferation before, during and after repatriation need to be considered.

Steps to Take before boarding:

·Strengthen bilateral communication, coordination and planning with competent authorities before departure.

·The aircraft should be adequately staffed with medical personnel to accommodate the anticipated number of nationals and equipped with appropriate PPE and equipment/supplies to respond to in–flight diseases.

·The non–medical crew of the aircraft should be properly briefed and equipped and pay attention to signs and symptoms to detect symptomatic passengers of the NCoV.

·Exit screening, such as temperature measurements and questionnaires, should be carried out before departure in order to detect symptoms early. Screening results should be Shared with recipient countries.

·It is recommended that travel of suspected sick passengers detected through exit screening be delayed for further assessment and treatment.

审校员：何丽霞

审校时间：2020.3.21

五、参考译文

For countries that have decided to repatriate their nationals from Wuhan City, Hubei province, the following key considerations need to be made, in order to ensure the health and wellbeing of those involved in the repatriation. In addition, measures aimed at bolstering national preparedness capacities to prevent the further spread before, during and after repatriation need to be considered.

Measures to be adopted before embarkation:

·Advanced bilateral communication, coordination, and planning with the responsible authorities before departure.

·The aircraft should be properly staffed with sufficient medical personnel to accommodate the number of nationals anticipated, and that they are outfitted with appropriate PPE and equipment/supplies to respond to illness on route.

•The non-medical crew of the aircraft should be properly briefed and outfitted, as well as aware of the signs and symptoms to detect symptomatic passengers for NCoV.

•Exitscreening, forexampletemperaturemeasurement and a questionnaire, should be conducted before departure for the early detection of symptoms. Screening results should be shared with the receiving country.

•It is advised to delay the travel of the suspected ill travelers detected through exit screening to be referred for further evaluation and treatment.

第五节 翻译实务评析

一、词法分析

旅游文本具有极强的渲染性，其目的是宣传旅游景点及服务，从而说服读者消费。基于此目的，旅游文本多使用描述性的动词、名词、形容词等，且词汇涉及文化、政治、经济、民俗等各个领域。原文（汉译英）涉及医学领域，出现较多的缩略词和专有名词，由于目标语读者并非医学领域专业人士，因此译者应补充全称加以说明，以便读者更加直观清晰地获取信息。例如：原文（汉译英）中，将2019-NCoV译为“2019年新型冠状病毒”，Public Health Emergency of International Concern（PHEIC）译为“国际公共卫生紧急事件（PHEIC）”。

二、句法分析

在英语的旅游文本中常见长难句，例如，在原文（汉译英）中，“对于决定从湖北省武汉市遣返其国民的国家，为确保遣返人员的健康和福祉，需要考虑以下关键因素”英语将汉语三个短句整合为一句，译为“For countries that have decided to repatriate their nationals from Wuhan City, Hubei province, the following key considerations need to be made, in order to ensure the health and well-being of those involved in the repatriation.”译文由“that”引起定语从句，后面的“have decided to repatriate their nationals from Wuhan City ”用来修饰countries——特指“决定从湖北省武汉市遣返其国民的国家”；汉语多主动，英语多被动，这里的汉语是“需要考虑以下关键因素”，英译为“key considerations need to be made”。

三、语篇分析

作为一篇完整、逻辑清楚、衔接畅通的文章，同一事物名称，除代指以外，全文应当统一。例如：在原文（汉译英）中，WHO全文皆译为全称“世界卫生组织”，并未由于多次出现而省译为“世卫组织”。汉语表达缺少逻辑标志词汇，各句、各段、甚至文章的逻辑关系都需凭借读者个人理解及感悟。而在英译中，往往需要将汉语潜在的逻辑关系显性化。例如：在原文（汉译英）第一段中，两个句子之间没有出现任何关系词，而在译文中加入了“In addition”将两个句子之间的逻辑关系表面化。英语常使用代词代指前文出现过的内容，以增加语篇连贯性，也可避免同一名词在文中反复出现，拖沓冗长，而汉语习惯以各式别称或者具有代指含义的词语来代替，譬如“其，之”等。例如：在原文（英译汉）中，“Following that determination”中的“that”代指上文中的“世界卫生组织总干事宣布2019-NCoV新型冠状病毒的爆发为国际公共卫生紧急事件（PHEIC）”这项声明，而译文将其处理为“根据这一决定”。

【课外拓展】

请你与团队进行角色扮演，模拟带领外宾在红色文化城市进行旅游。

文献参考

[1]董丽颖．翻译亦营销——以营销为导向的旅游目的地官方网页翻译探究[J]．中国翻译,2013,34(02):109-112.

[2]黄立波．基于专门用途语料库的翻译研究综述[J]．北京第二外国语学院学报,2017,39(02):70-82+136.

[3]黄忠廉．翻译项目管理[M]．北京:国防工业出版社,2014.

[4]李德超,王克非．新型双语旅游语料库的研制和应用[J]．现代外语,2010,33(01):46-54+109.

[5]吕政．跨文化视域下的旅游广告翻译研究[J]．上海翻译,2016(01):43-46.

[6]牛新生．关于旅游景点名称翻译的文化反思——兼论旅游景点翻译的规范化研究[J]．中国翻译,2013,34(03):99-104.

[7]桑龙扬．旅游景点名称翻译的原则与方法——以庐山等旅游景区为例[J]．中国科技翻译,2011,24(04):46-49.

[8]唐芳,李德超．基于语料库的汉译旅游文本“翻译固有型”词汇特征研究[J].

解放军外国语学院学报,2016,39(03):117-124.

[9]王爱琴. 入乎其内,出乎其外——论汉英旅游翻译过程中思维的转换与重写[J]. 中国翻译,2012,33(01):98-102.

[10]杨红英. 旅游景点翻译的规范化研究——陕西省地方标准《公共场所公示语英文译写规范:旅游》的编写启示[J]. 中国翻译,2011,32(04):64-68.

[11]邹建玲. 旅游翻译研究1998-2012年综述——基于人文类核心期刊语料分析[J]. 中国科技翻译,2013,26(04):48-51+60.

[12]张志祥. 旅游翻译中的交际规范[J]. 上海翻译,2017(02):13-16.

第十三章　学术翻译

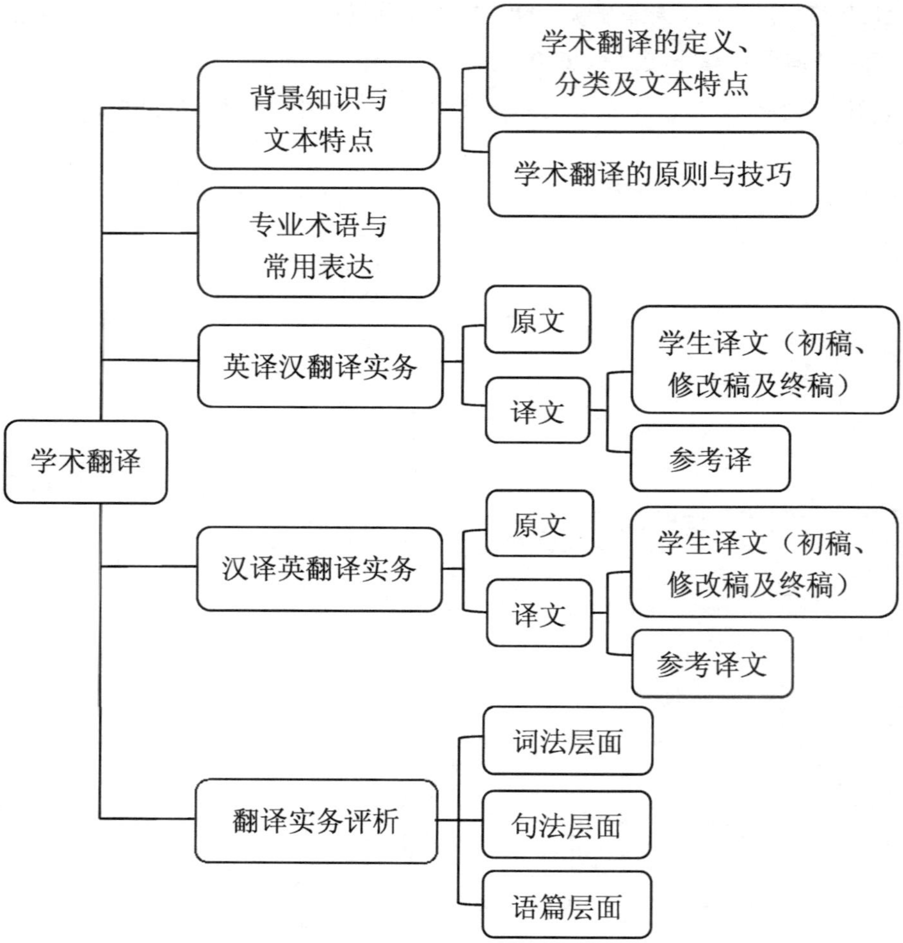
学术翻译
背景知识与文本特点
学术翻译的定义、分类及文本特点
学术翻译的原则与技巧
专业术语与常用表达
英译汉翻译实务
原文
译文
学生译文（初稿、修改稿及终稿）
参考译
汉译英翻译实务
原文
译文
学生译文（初稿、修改稿及终稿）
参考译文
翻译实务评析
词法层面
句法层面
语篇层面

第一节　背景知识与文本特点

一、学术翻译定义、分类及文本特点

学术翻译，即指对于学术类著作的翻译。学术翻译作为翻译研究领域的一个重要组成部分，着重于意识形态的思考，对问题进行概念性分析。从研究领域来说学术翻译大致可以分为两类：交际意义上的学术翻译和科学意义上的学术翻译。学术文本具有鲜明的文本特点，即科学性、严谨性、抽象性与层次性。科学性是学术文本的根本特征，其内容及用语都反映着客观事实，忠于客观事物的本质及其发展规律；严谨性是指学术文本用语十分准确，对遣词造句的精准度要求极高，不允许出现任何错误；抽象性即指学术文本的部分语言较为专业化、小众化，体现着特定的时代内涵及特色；层次性是指学术文本的结构层次十分鲜明，逻辑非常紧密，前后文的衔接十分紧凑。

二、学术翻译的原则与技巧

由于学术文本独特的文体特征，进行学术翻译时需要遵循一定的原则与技巧。首先，学术文本的翻译必须确保准确性。由于学术文本旨在呈现或传送特定领域的知识，具有普及大众或某些特定受众的作用，所以学术文本的翻译不允许错误的产生。其次，学术文本的翻译必须确保专业性。学术文本所反映的内容应是相关学科专业系统的理论化知识，它反映的必然是某一领域的前沿化知识，所以必须确保译文呈现的专业性。此外，学术翻译必须确保规范性。规范是严谨的体现，学术文本作为高度严谨的文本，它的翻译过程必须正确规范。基于此，学术翻译可以遵循直译与意译相结合、增译与释译相辅助的翻译技巧。值得注意的是，一般情况下，学术文本不会采取省译的翻译技巧，这也是由于其文本的特殊性决定的。

第二节　专业术语与常用表达

ST	TT
1.显著性检验	significance testing
2.尾符	end punctuation marks
3.显著性差异	difference significant
4.标准差	standard deviation
5.统计量数	statistical measure
6.形成性评价	formative assessment
7.标准参照性测试	criterion referenced test
8.考生	examinee
9.评分者,阅卷者	grader
10.评分者间信度	inter-rater reliability
11.常模参照性测试	norm-referenced test
12.因果解释	causal explanation
13.管道隐喻	conduit metaphor
14.语篇语义学	discourse semantics
15.经验意义	experiential meaning
16.全局语境	global context
17.笔迹学	graphology
18.概念意义	ideational meaning
19.惯用语	idiomatic expression
20.整体法	a holistic method
21.分析法	an analytical method
22.区分度	discrimination
23.档案袋评价	Portfolio assessments
24.斯皮尔曼等级相关系数	Spearman rank correlation coefficients

续表

ST	TT
25.表现能力测试	Performance test
26.评分员	rater
27.互动社会语言学	Sociolinguistics
28.会话分析	Conversation Analysis
29.联络口译	Liaison Interpreting
30.社会学	Sociology
31.语言学	Linguistics
32.词汇语义学	Lexico-semantics
33.会话管理	Conversational management
34.语篇管理	Discourse management
35.条件反射	conditioned reflex
36.混淆变量	confounding cariable
37.退出能力	exit level competence
38.一般心理能力	general mental ability
39.元分析	meta-analysis
40.元认知能力	meta-cognition
41.抽象分析法	method of abstract analysis
42.心理状态	mental state
43.神经语言学	neurolinguistics
44.组织心理学	organizational psychology
45.语言沟通	the interactional mode
46.理解诠释	the interpretive mode
47.表达演示	the presentational mode
48.施为能力	illocutionary competence
49.视觉变量	visual variation
50.量化对比分析	comparative quantitative analysis

第三节　英译汉翻译实务

一、原文

Translation scholars have long noted that assessment, a key component in translator training, is performed in a generally arbitrary manner. The use of corpora to document differences within language pairs, however, can provide an empirical basis for the formulation of assessment tools. The present study, based on data collected from Russian and English comparable corpora organized by text type, offers a case study in the development of an assessment tool designed to evaluate three isolatable, but nevertheless frequently ignored, features of textual cohesion: punctuation, sentencing, and paragraphing. Because novice translators tend to focus on the level of the word or phrase, ignoring textual elements occurring above the sentence level, focusing assessment on such textual elements can encourage novices to consider the target text globally, as a professional product composed of various features above and beyond lexis. A granular tool for assessing punctuation in Russian>English texts is provided, which can be replicated for other language pairs as well.

二、学生译文初稿

很长时间以来，翻译学者们便注意到，评估是译者培训一个重要组成部分，但评估工具较为随意。然而，利用语料库确定语言对之间的差异可以为评估工具的制定提供实证数据。本研究基于俄语和英语语料库中的文本类型，为评估标点、句子和段落三个独立但逐渐被忽略的语篇衔接功能设计评估工具提供个案研究。由于初学翻译的人一般注重词汇或短语的翻译，从而忽略了句子层面的文本要素，专业产品包括很多此法之外的层面，所以基于文本元素进行评估可以鼓励初学者全面思考目的语文本。现已有一种评估俄语>英语文本标点符号的更精确的工具，其他语言也可参考这种评估工具进行评估。

——译员：张胜霞

三、学生译文修改稿

长时间以来，翻译学者们已然注意到，评估是译者培训一个重要环节，但评估工具的选择较为随意。然而，利用语料库确定语言对之间的差异可以为评估工具的制定提供实证数据。本研究基于俄语和英语语料库中的文本类型，为标点、句子和段落这三个语篇衔接功能设计评估工具提供个案研究，三者各自独立但人们对其日益忽略。由于翻译初学者一般注重词汇或短语的翻译，从而忽略了句子层面的文本要素，专业产品涵盖众多此法之外的层面，所以基于文本要素进行评估可以鼓励初学者全面思考目的语文本。现已有一种用于评估俄语>英语文本标点符号的更为精确的工具，其他语言也可参考这种评估工具进行评估。

删除[A]：很

删除[A]：便

删除[A]：组成部分

删除[A]：评估

删除[A]：独立但逐渐被忽略的

删除[A]：初学翻译的人

删除[A]：包括很多

删除[A]：元

删除[A]：，

审校人：马丽

审校时间：2020.5.15

四、学生译文终稿

长时间以来，翻译学者们已然注意到，评估是译者培训的一个重要环节，但评估工具的选择较为随意。然而，利用语料库确定语言对之间的差异可以为评估工具的制定提供实证数据。本研究基于俄语和英语语料库中的文本类型，为标点、句子和段落这三个语篇衔接功能设计评估工具提供个案研究，三者各自独立但人们对其日益忽略。由于翻译初学者一般注重词汇或短语的翻译，从而忽略了句子层面的文本要素，专业产品涵盖众多此法之外的层面，所以基于文本要素进行评估可以鼓励初学者全面思考目的语文本。现已有一种用于评估俄语>英语文本标点符号的更为精确的工具，其他语言也可参考这种评估工具进行评估。

五、参考译文

翻译学家们早就注意到这一点：评估作为译者培训的重要环节，其方式较为随意。但是，利用语料库确定语对之间的差异可为评估工具的制定提供实证数据。本研究基于俄语和英语语料库中的文本类型，对用于标点、句子和段落的评估工具的发展进行个案研究。这三个语篇衔接功能相互独立，因此人们对此日渐忽略。由于翻译初学者一般注重词汇或短语层面的翻译，从而忽略了句子层面的文本要素，因此，关注这类文本要素的评估可以启发初学者们全面考量目的语文本，将其视为一项包含多种词法特征的专业产品。目前已有一种用于评估俄语>英语文本标点符号的更为精确的工具，其他语言也可对此参考并进行评估。

第四节　汉译英翻译实务

一、原文

因为语料库编纂由人工完成，且时间和资源有限，所以设定每个语料库的长度为2万词。需要指出的是，如果使用更大的语料库，那么数据结果也会更可靠。虽然2万词的语料库能够反映既定文本类型的总体趋势，特别是每个句子都会有标点的分数，但是我们需要利用更大的语料库深入研究标点符号的使用。

研究句子和段落时，我们在语料库中新增了文本类型，语料库得到进一步发展。除社论以外，语料库还增加了国际新闻文章（选自《纽约时报》）以及当代文学类文章。所有的社论和国际新闻文章选自2005年到2006年间。文章根据内容随机挑选。两个语料库都为文学语料库。网上随机挑选的文章节本的发行日期为2004年到2006年。不同文章的数量为20篇（例如，120篇文章，总词数为116140个词）。新增的文本类型提高了语料库数据的可信度。

二、学生译文初稿

Because corpus compilation is done manually, and time and resources are limited, the length of each corpus is assumed to be 20,000 words. It should be pointed out that the data results would also be more reliable if a larger corpus was used. Although a corpus of 20,000 words can reflect the general trend of a given text type, especially with punctuation marks for each sentence, we need to use a larger corpus to study punctuation usage in depth.

When we study sentences and paragraphs, we add text types to the corpus, which further develops the corpus. In addition to editorials, the corpus also includes international news articles (selected from The New York Times) and contemporary literature articles. All editorials and international news articles are from 2005 and 2006. Articles are randomly selected according to their content. Both corpora are literary corpora. The online editions of the randomly selected articles were published between 2004 and 2006.

The number of different articles is 20 (for example, 120 articles with a total of 116140 words). The new text types enhance the credibility of corpus data.

——译员：陈春

三、学生译文修改稿

Because corpus compilation is done manually, as well as time and resources are limited, each corpus is set as 20,000 words. It should be pointed out that the results would also be more reliable if a larger corpus was used. Although a corpus of 20,000 words can reflect the general trend of a given text type, especially with punctuation marks for each sentence, we still need to use a larger corpus to study punctuation usage in depth.

When we study sentences and paragraphs, other new text types are added to the corpus, which further develops the corpus. In addition to editorials, the corpus also includes international news articles (selected from the *New York Times*) and contemporary literature articles. All editorials and international news articles are from 2005 and 2006. Articles are randomly selected according to content. Both corpora are literary corpora. The online editions of the randomly selected articles were published between 2004 and 2006. There are 20 different articles (for example, 120 articles with a total of 116,140 words). The new text types enhance the credibility of corpus data.

删除[A]: and

删除[A]: the length of

删除[A]: assumed to be

删除[A]: data

删除[A]: we add

删除[A]: T

设置格式[A]: 字体: 倾斜

删除[A]: their

删除[A]: The number of

删除[A]: is 20

审校人：马丽

审校时间：2020.5.15

四、学生译文终稿

Because corpus compilation is done manually, as well as time and resources are limited, each corpus is set as 20,000 words. It should be pointed out that the results would also be more reliable if a larger corpus was used. Although a corpus of 20,000 words can reflect the general trend of a given text type, especially with punctuation marks for each sentence, we still need to use a larger corpus to study punctuation usage in depth.

When we study sentences and paragraphs, other new text types are added to the corpus, which further develops the corpus. In addition to editorials, the corpus also includes international news articles (selected from the New York Times) and contemporary literature articles. All editorials and international news articles are from 2005 and 2006. Articles are randomly selected according to content. Both corpora are literary corpora. The online editions of the randomly selected articles were published between 2004 and 2006. There are 20 different articles (for example, 120 articles with a total of 116,140 words). The new text types enhance the credibility of corpus data.

五、参考译文

Since the corpus compilation was performed manually and with limited time and resources, the length of each corpus is only 20,000 words. It should be noted that the statistical results would have been more reliable if larger corpora had been used. A further investigation of punctuation use in larger English and Russian corpora is therefore desirable, although a 20,000 word corpus should reflect the general tendencies in a given text type, particularly in regard to punctuation marks, which of course appear in every sentence.

For the study of sentencing and paragraphing, our corpus was developed further, with new text-types added. In addition to editorials, international news articles (from the same newspapers, The New York Times) and contemporary literary texts were included as additional corpora. All the editorials and international news articles were published in 2005-2006. The articles were selected randomly, regardless of their content. The same holds true for the literary corpora. The publication dates of the randomly selected excerpts of books availably online range from 2004 to 2006. The number of different texts in each category was 20(i.e., 120 texts, totaling 116,140 words). The increased number of text types improves the reliability of the data elicited from the corpus.

第五节　翻译实务评析

一、词法分析

词法是翻译过程中的最小单位，对于词法的分析，既关乎到句意的理解，又涉及到对句子结构的初步把握。本次翻译实践原文本皆为学术文本，其词法特征就是专业术语较多，熟词生意的情况也较为常见。综合来看，原文本用词比较灵活多变，没有拘泥于某一类词的运用之中。同时，由于学术文本的特征所限，原文本词法运用十分严谨，需要译者考虑到文本的特殊性，在具体的语境之下对词汇进行恰当翻译。如原文本（英译汉）中出现了“component”一词，它的本意是“成分、组件、元件”，但结合它出现的具体语境“a key component in translator training”就会发现不能选择其本意进行直译，需要将其翻译为了“环节”“步骤”“内容”等词，这也体现了学术翻译用词的科学严谨性。

二、句法分析

句子是学术文本的基本组成单位。由于学术文本旨在陈述客观事实，传递实际知识，所以在时态来看，原文本多偏向使用一般现在时，从语态来看更多地使用了被动语态，这些时态语态特征正是学术翻译中需要格外注意的地方。如原文（汉译英）中，“我们在语料库中新增了文本类型”，在源语中该句为主动语态，但在译文中译者有意将其转换为了被动语态 “other new text types are added to the corpus”，这样能够增强译文的客观性，更加贴合学术文本的表达习惯和行文特色、用语风格。

三、语篇分析

从语篇角度来看，学术文本结构十分紧密，文本框架十分完整，译者在翻译时一定不能忽略前后文的衔接，也不能忽视文章的整体逻辑性。如原文（英译汉及汉译英）中多使用连接词和关系词，在翻译的过程中不可丢失，例如译者在本篇英译汉的翻译实践中增译了“由于”“从而”“因为”等衔接前后文、表明前后逻辑关系的词，这样才能清楚地展示出学术文本坚实的结构框架，才能使得前后文本不脱离，更加体现其专业性和科学性。

【课外拓展】

为完成某一科研项目，你打算与国内外翻译学家进行一次深度访谈，请与你的团队模拟情境，进行学术人物的访谈翻译。

文献参考

[1]陈冰．浅论学术翻译中的译者主体性．英语广场(学术研究)．2014(12)．

[2]陈生梅．中国学术翻译研究20年．兰州大学学报(社会科学版)．2011(07):149-154．

[3]范梦栩．学术翻译研究的现状与展望[J]．民族翻译．2020(02)

[4]郭庆民．从批评话语理论的核心理念看英汉学术翻译[J]．国外理论动态．2017(03)

[5]黄忠廉．翻译项目管理[M]．北京:国防工业出版社,2014.

[6]侯晶晶．试论近30年中国学术翻译的形态嬗变．南京师大学报(社会科学版)．2007(05)

[7]路阳．学术文本翻译的基本策略探究[J]．北方文学．2019(14)

[8]孙周兴．学术翻译的几个原则——以海德格尔著作之汉译为例[J]．中国翻译．2013(04)

[9]吴文安．学术翻译之难——以本雅明《译者的任务》选段为例[J]．中国翻译．2014(03)

[10]周鹤,张保国．中国学术"走出去"的翻译之道——以农史学家石声汉的学术外译为例[J]．上海翻译．2021(01)

[11]周领顺．学术翻译研究与批评纲论[J]．外语研究．2008(1):78-84.

第十四章　工程翻译

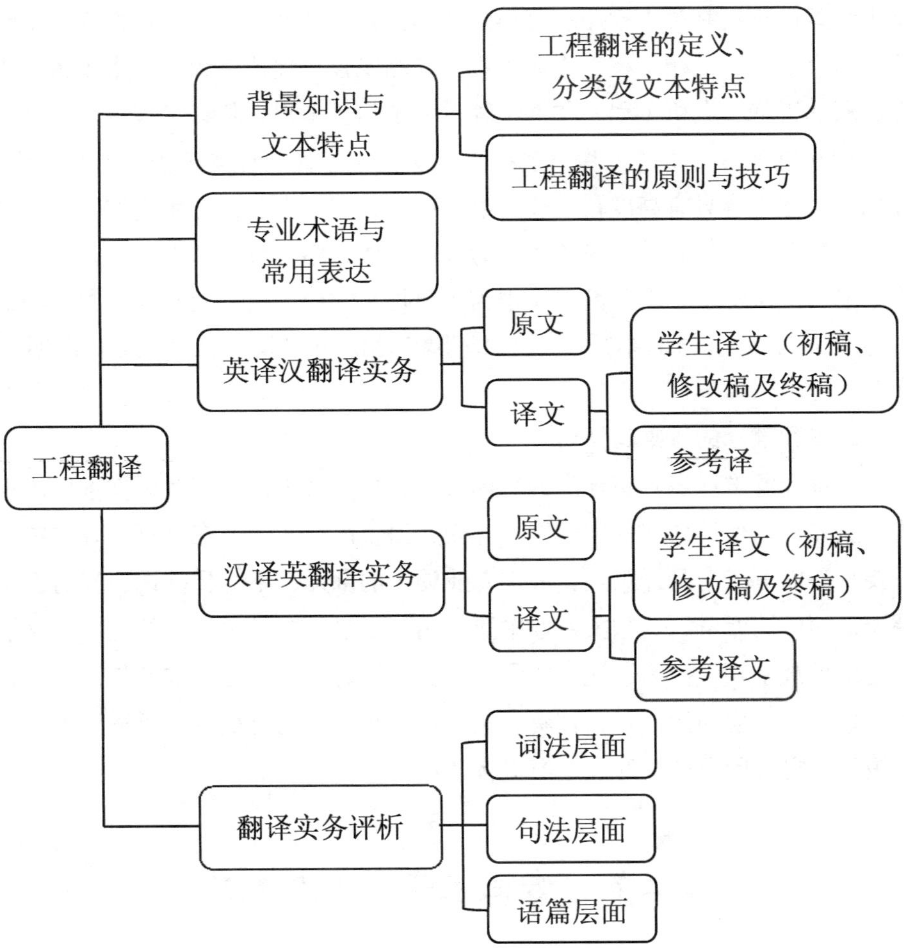
工程翻译
背景知识与文本特点
工程翻译的定义、分类及文本特点
工程翻译的原则与技巧
专业术语与常用表达
英译汉翻译实务
原文
译文
学生译文（初稿、修改稿及终稿）
参考译
汉译英翻译实务
原文
译文
学生译文（初稿、修改稿及终稿）
参考译文
翻译实务评析
词法层面
句法层面
语篇层面

第一节 背景知识与文本特点

一、工程翻译定义、分类及文本特点

工程翻译是指有关工程原理介绍的文本翻译，涉及面广，专业性强。工程翻译涉及冶金工程、机械工程、交通工程、基因工程、地质工程、土木工程、农业工程、园林工程、电机工程、软件工程、电子信息工程、材料工程、航空航天工程、水利水电工程、采矿工程、选矿工程、物流工程、环境工程、安全工程等。工程翻译文本内容具有高度科学性，语言严谨，用词专业，专用名词较多；语言具有严密准确性，句式结构较长，多为被动构式；结构具有清晰的条理性，文本结构严谨，层次清晰。工程翻译文本为了要把事物说明白，就必须把握事物的特征，进而揭示出事物的本质属性，即不仅要说明“是什么”，还要说明“为什么”。

二、工程翻译的原则与技巧

工程翻译要求译者具备极高的翻译素养，能有效查询并理解原文本中出现的相关专业知识，保证译文的准确性，并使其语言简洁明了。在进行工程文本翻译时，要掌握以下三个翻译难点：一、专业词汇的翻译，不可根据词典找的意思直接翻译，而应该参考原文相关专业中所使用的术语；二、被动句的翻译，汉语中应避免出现被字句，而为了让句式灵活，在英译时可适当使用被动句；三、长难句的翻译，首先应通读原句，理解含义，再对长难句进行划分，可适当拆分成几个中短句，再按照目的语的表达习惯将其整合。

第二节 专业术语与常用表达

ST	TT
1. 精整	finishing
2. 轧制	rolling
3. 均热炉	soaking pits

续表

ST	TT
4.成品车间	finishing shop
5.堆垛	stacking up
6.酸洗	pickling
7.退火	annealing
8.宽缘钢梁	wide-flanged beams
9.电磁的	electromagnetic
10.多孔喷枪	multi-nozzle lamce
11.焊条芯	core wire
12.脱氧剂	deoxidizer
13.连铸机	continuous caster
14.真空炉顶	vacuum furnace roof
15.移动感应加热器	mobile induction heater
16.电弧炉	electric arc furnace
17.变压器	transformer
18.涡流	eddy current
19.绕组	winding
20.磁通	flux
21.交流电压源	alternating-voltage source
22.交变磁通	alternating flux
23.匝数	the number of turns
24.铁心变压器	iron-core transformer
25.磁路	magnetic circuit
26.硅钢	silicon steel
27.高导磁性	high permeability
28.铁磁材料	ferromagnetic material
29.混凝土	concrete

续表

ST	TT
30.恒荷载	the dead load
31.活荷载	the live load
32.硅酸盐水泥	portland cement
33.合金	alloy
34.石灰石	limestone
35.抗张强度	tensile strength
36.可塑性	plasticity
37.抗压强度	strength under compression
38.和易性	workability
39.耐用性	durability
40.反应性颗粒	reactive particles
41.矿物添加剂	mineral admixtures
42.减水剂	water-reducing admixture
43.水化水泥浆	hydrated cement paste
44.离析	segregation
45.智能运输系统	Intelligent Transportation System
46.电子收费系统	Electronic Toll Collection
47.中心主机	Central host
48.无线电频率	Radio frequency
49.结构混凝土	structural concrete
50.时变电压	Time-varying voltage

第三节　英译汉翻译实务

一、原文

Equation, e=dλ/dt, can be used to determine the voltages induced by time-varying magnetic fields. Electromagnetic energy conversion occurs when changes in the flux linkage λ result from mechanical motion. In rotating machines, voltages are generated in windings or groups of coils by rotating these windings mechanically through a magnetic field, by mechanically rotating a magnetic field past the winding, or by designing the magnetic circuit so that the reluctance varies with rotation of the rotor. By any of these methods, the flux linking a specific coil is changed cyclically, and a time-varying voltage is generated.

A set of such coils connected together is typically referred to as an armature winding. In general, the term armature winding is used to refer to a winding or a set of windings on a rotating machine which carry AC currents. In AC machines such as synchronous or induction machines, the armature winding is typically on the stationary portion of the motor referred to as the stator, in which case these windings may also be referred to as stator windings.

二、学生译文初稿

方程式e=dλ/dt可被用来确定由时变电磁场产生的感应电势。电磁能的转换发生于机械运动导致磁链λ发生变化之时。在旋转电机中，电压产生于绕组或几组线圈中，通过机械旋转绕组、经过绕组机械旋转磁场和设计磁路，让磁阻随着转子的转动而变化，循环改变连接特定线圈的磁通，并产生时变电压。

一组这样连接起来的线圈就是典型的电枢绕组。通常来说，术语“电枢绕组”是指旋转电机上带有交流电流的一个或一组绕组。在交流电机中，比如同步电机或感应式电机等，电枢绕组通常放置固定部分，而这一处可能被称为定子绕组。

——译员：王婷婷

三、学生译文修改稿

方程式 e=dλ/dt 可用来确定由时变电磁场产生的感应电势。当机械运动导致磁链λ发生变化时，会发生电磁能的转换。在旋转电机中，绕组或几组线圈可以通过以下三种方式产生电压：在磁场内机械旋转绕组、经过绕组机械旋转磁场和设计磁路，让磁阻随着转子的转动而变化。以上三种方式都可以循环改变连接特定线圈的磁通，并产生时变电压。

一组这样连接起来的线圈就是典型的电枢绕组。通常来说，术语“电枢绕组”是指旋转电机上带有交流电流的一个或一组绕组。比如同步电机或感应式电机等的交流电机中，电枢绕组通常放置在被称为定子绕组的固定部分。

审校人：乔婷

审校时间：2020.6.10

删除[T]：被

删除[T]：发生于机械运动导致磁链λ发生变化之时。

删除[T]：电压产生于

删除[T]：中，

删除[T]：，

删除[T]：在交流电机中，比如同步电机或

删除[T]：，而这一处可能被称为定子绕组

设置格式[T]：右

四、学生译文终稿

方程式 e=dλ/dt 可用来确定时变电磁场的感应电势。当机械运动导致磁链λ发生变化时，会发生电磁能的转换。在旋转电机中，绕组或几组线圈可以通过以下三种方式产生电压：在磁场内机械旋转绕组；经过绕组机械旋转磁场；设计磁路，让磁阻随着转子的转动而变化。以上三种方式都可以循环改变连接特定线圈的磁通，并产生时变电压。

一组这样连接起来的线圈就是典型的电枢绕组。通常来说，术语“电枢绕组”是指旋转电机上带有交流电流的一个或一组绕组。比如同步电机或感应式电机等的交流电机中，电枢绕组通常放置在被称为定子绕组的固定部分。

审校人：乔婷

审校时间：2020.6.10

五、参考译文

我们可以用式 e=dλ/dt 来确定时变磁场的感应电势。当机械运动引起磁链λ变化时，机电能量的转换就会伴随发生。在旋转电机中，绕组或者线圈组中感应电势的产生是通过下述方法之一来实现的：使绕组在磁场中做机械旋转；或者使磁场做机械旋转掠过绕组；或者把磁路的磁阻设计成随转子转动而变化。不论哪

一种方法，与特定线圈匝链的磁通都会周期变化，并且产生时变电势。

习惯上把连在一起的一组这样的线圈称为电枢绕组。电枢绕组这个术语通常是指旋转电机中流过交流电流的一个或者一组线圈。在同步电机和感应电机这样的交流电机中，电枢绕组一般位于被称为定子的不动部件上，这时电枢绕组也称为定子绕组。

第四节　汉译英翻译实务

一、原文

从本质上说，一台变压器由两个或多个绕组组成，互磁通使绕组间相耦合。如果其中一个绕组（称为一次侧）连接到交流电压源，将会产生一个交变磁通，其幅值取决于一次侧电压的大小、所施加电压的频率和绕组的匝数。这一互磁通将匝链另一绕组（称为二次侧）并在其中感应电势，其幅值取决于二次侧绕组的匝数及互磁通的幅值和频率。适当选择一、二次侧绕组的匝数配合，几乎可以得到任何想要的电压比或变比。

变压器作用的本质，是仅需要存在匝链两个绕组的时变互磁通。这一作用同样可以出现在通过空气耦合的两个绕组上，但用铁或其他铁磁材料作为铁心会使绕组间的耦合更加有效，因为大部分磁通将被限制在明确的、高导磁性的匝链绕组的路径中。这类变压器通常称为铁心变压器，变压器大多属于此类型，后面的讨论几乎都是针对铁心变压器。

二、学生译文初稿

Essentially, a transformer is made up of two or more windings. And it can be coupled by mutual magnetic flux. If a winding is connected to an alternating-voltage source, then an alternating flux will be produced whose amplitude will depend on the primary voltage, the frequency of acted voltage and the number of winding turns. The mutual flux will link the other winding and interact potentials in it whose amplitude will depend on the secondary’ s turns, the amplitude and the frequency of the mutual flux. Any ratio of voltage or transformer can be obtained by proper selections of the primary and the secondary’ s turns.

The operating principal of transformer only needs the time-varying mutual flux between two windings of the linkage, which can exist in two windings coupled on air as well. However, the couple between windings will be more effective with iron or other magnetic material as the iron-core. Because most of flux will be limited on the routine of a certain linkage winding with high permeability. Transformers as described above is called as iron-core transformer, which will be mainly focused in the following discussion for it is the most common kind of transformers.

——译员：陈春

三、学生译文修改稿

Essentially, there are two or more windings included in a transformer. And it canb be coupled by mutual magnetic flux. If a winding, the Primary, is connected to an alternating-voltage source, then an alternating flux will be produced with an amplitude depending on the primary voltage, the frequency of acted voltage and the number of winding turns. The mutual flux will link the other winding, the Secondary, and interact potentials in it whose amplitude will depend on the secondary' s turns, the amplitude and the frequency of the mutual flux. Any ratio of voltage or transformer can be obtained by proper selections of the Primary and the Secondary' s turns.

The operating principal of transformer only requires the time-varying mutual flux between two windings of the linkage, which can exist in two windings coupled on air as well. However, the couple between windings will be more effective with iron or other magnetic material as the iron-core. Because most of flux will be limited on the routine of a certain linkage winding with high permeability. Transformers as described above is called as iron-core transformer, which will be mainly focused in the following discussion for it is the most common kind of transformers.

审校人：乔婷

审校时间：2020.6.12

删除[T]: is made up of two or more windings. And it can be coupled by

删除[T]: whose

删除[T]: will depend

删除[T]: p

删除[T]: s

删除[T]: need

删除[T]: s

删除[T]:

设置格式[T]: 缩进: 首行缩进: 2 字符

设置格式[T]: 右, 缩进: 首行缩进: 2 字符

四、学生译文终稿

Essentially, there are two or more windings included in a transformer. And it can be coupled by mutual magnetic flux. If a winding, the Primary, is connected to an alternating-voltage source, then an alternating flux will be produced with an amplitude depending on the primary voltage, the frequency of acted voltage and the number of winding turns. The mutual flux will link the other winding, the Secondary, and interact potentials in it whose amplitude will depend on the Secondary' s turns, the amplitude and the frequency of the mutual flux. Any ratio of voltage or transformer can be obtained by proper selections of the Primary and the Secondary' s turns.

The operating principal of transformer only requires the time-varying mutual flux between two windings of the linkage, which can exist in two windings coupled on air as well. However, the couple between windings will be more effective with iron or other magnetic material as the iron-core. Because most of flux will be limited on the routine of a certain linkage winding with high permeability. Transformers as described above is called as iron-core transformer, which will be mainly focused in the following discussion for it is the most common kind of transformers.

审校人：乔婷

审校时间：2020.6.12

五、参考译文

Essentially, a transformer consists of two or more windings coupled by mutual magnetic flux. If one of these windings, the primary, is connected to an alternating-voltage source, an alternating flux will be produced whose amplitude will depend on the primary voltage, the frequency of the applied voltage, and the number of turn. The mutual flux will link the other winding, the secondary, and will induce a voltage in it whose value will depend on the number of secondary turns as well as the magnitude of the mutual flux and the frequency. By properly proportioning the number of primary and secondary turns, almost any desired voltage ration, or ratio of transformation, can be obtained.

The essence of transformer action requires only the existence of time-varying mutual flux linking two windings. Such action can occur for two windings coupled through air, but coupling between the windings can be made much more effectively using a core of iron or other ferromagnetic material, because most of the flux is then confined to a definite, high-permeability path linking the windings. Such a transformer is commonly called an iron-core transformer. Most transformers are of this type. The following discussion is concerned almost wholly with iron-core transformers.

第五节 翻译实务评析

一、词法分析

两篇原文均属于电机工程的范围。英译汉原文解释了方程式e=dλ/dt的基本原理、电枢绕组的定义以及二次绕组的相关原理。汉译英原文则介绍了关于变压器的相关基本知识，包括变压器的定义及其作用的本质以及两种基本类型——芯式结构和壳式结构的基本原理。原文包含大量的专有名词，为保证译文的准确性，译者必须利用好一切资源来查证专有名词的内涵及在文中的特定含义。

二、句法分析

原文使用了大量连接词，句与句之间的关系较明确，以中短句居多。翻译时，应整合句子关系，避免出现句子冗长的情况，保留说明文的简要性。此外，为保证原文的客观性，译者应当灵活使用被动语态。

如：（1）ST-- Equation, e=dλ/dt, can be used to determine the voltages induced by time-varying magnetic

TT --方程式e=dλ/dt可用来确定时变电磁场的感应电势。

原文属于信息性（informative）文体，这类文体主要指科技文体、新闻文体、公文文体及论述文体。科技论文注重事理和活动的客观叙述（impersonal activity seen objectively），避免作者的主观臆断，因而常常避免提及施事。原文首句就使用了被动语态，在对比英汉表达差异之后，在翻译时不使用“被”字句，而是用“用来”体现原文中具有的被动语态。此外，原文中的“the voltages induced”不可直译为“由……引起的电势”，根据原文的背景知识，应该将其译为感应电势。

（2）ST-- 如果其中一个绕组（称为一次侧）连接到交流电压源，将会产生一个交变磁通，其幅值取决于一次侧电压的大小、所施加电压的频率和绕组的匝数。

TT -- If a winding, the primary, is connected with an alternating-voltage source, then an alternating flux will be produced whose amplitude will depend on the primary voltage, the frequency of acted voltage and the number of winding turns.

中国正常的被动式是必须把主事者说出的，因此原文在缺少主事者的情况下，用主动形式表达了被动语态。原文应该这么理解：一个绕组被连接到交流电压源；一个交变磁通将被产生。在翻译时，应将此句转换成被动语态。

三、语篇分析

原文属于信息型文本，信息型文本在生活中扮演着向读者传递信息的重要角色。信息型文本的翻译强调传达信息的真实性、准确性与可读性，同时信息型文本往往与源语的背景知识相关，有时会使用专业词汇，对译者的理解与表达能力提出了较高的要求，加大了翻译的难度。原文语篇中连接词较少，但逻辑清晰，层次分明，在理解上难度较小。

【课外拓展】

国外某机电工厂的工程师向学生解释变压器的工作原理，请你与团队模拟情境，进行翻译。

文献参考

[1]邓友生，蓝培华，李中林．土木工程英语翻译技巧[J]．中国科技翻译，2004，(04)：12-13+43.

[2]黄忠廉．翻译项目管理[M]．北京：国防工业出版社，2014.

[3]孔德亮．机电工程英语的特点及翻译[J]．中国科技翻译，2013，26(04)：5-7+27.

[4]罗天，吴弟菊．基于学习者语料库的工程汉英翻译之误译研究[J]．重庆交通大学学报(社会科学版)，2018，18(06)：113-118.

[5]穆凤良．从日常词汇到工程英语的切换与翻译[J]．中国科技翻译，2011，24(01)：5-9.

[6]肖凤华，殷白恩．人机共译交互平台在工程翻译中的运用——以传神语联网为例[J]．中国科技翻译，2019，32(03)：38-40+59.

[7]徐艳艳．翻译项目的组织和管理[J]．上海科技翻译，2002，(01)：27-29.

[8]赵运才．机电工程专业英语[M]．北京：北京大学出版社，2006.

[9]朱玉彬，陈坚林．基于语料库的计算机辅助翻译教学平台的理论构想与工程实践[J]．外语电化教学，2015，(04)：52-57.

第十五章　历史文献翻译

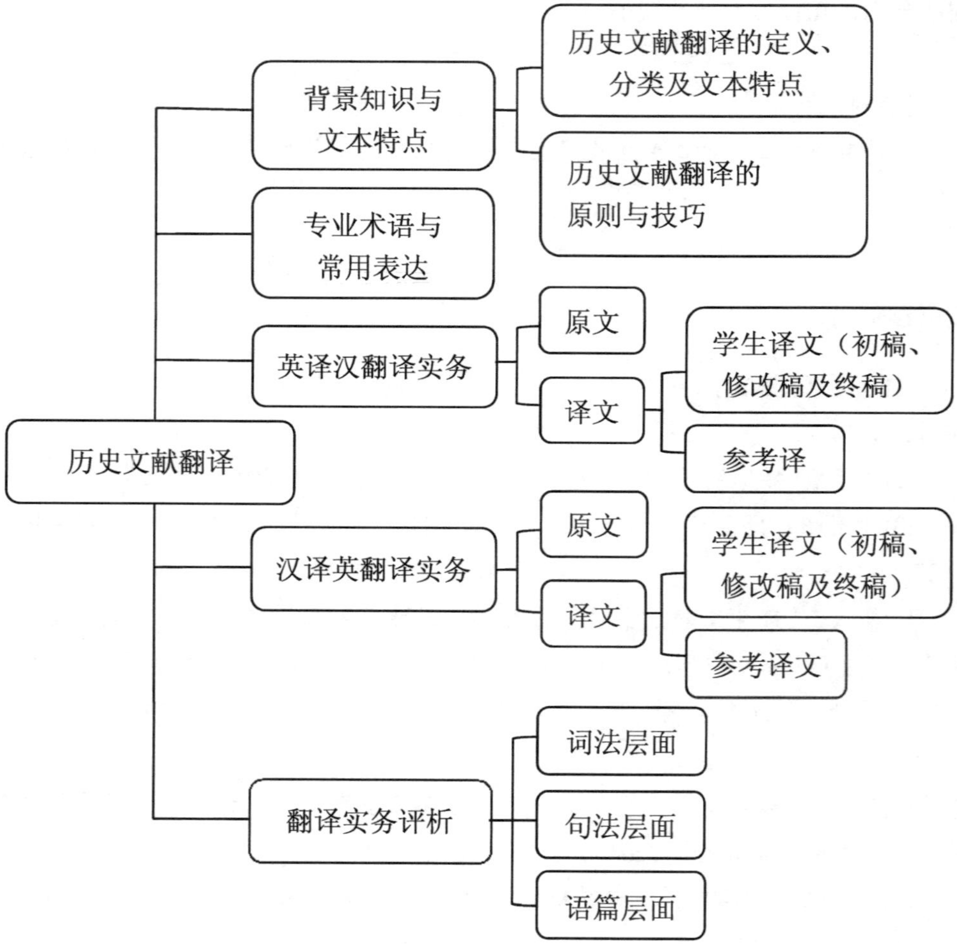
历史文献翻译
背景知识与文本特点
历史文献翻译的定义、分类及文本特点
历史文献翻译的原则与技巧
专业术语与常用表达
英译汉翻译实务
原文
译文
学生译文（初稿、修改稿及终稿）
参考译
汉译英翻译实务
原文
译文
学生译文（初稿、修改稿及终稿）
参考译文
翻译实务评析
词法层面
句法层面
语篇层面

第一节　背景知识与文本特点

一、历史文献翻译定义、分类及文本特点

在理解历史文献翻译定义之前，要先明确一切文献都是各种知识的记录，历史文献记载着发生在过去的事件。因此，历史文献的翻译是对所有记载了过去的知识、事件及人物的文本的翻译。根据资料的表现形式，历史文献翻译可划分为有意历史文献翻译与无意历史文献翻译。其中有意历史文献是指官方组织编写的史书和成文的历史著述、回忆录和公开报道等；无意历史文献是指官方遗留下来的文书档案、军事文件、私人信函或日记等。此外，根据文献的内容，历史文献翻译涉及人文、社科、自然等各个方面，含有大量文化负载词，且长难句和复合句较多。为证实某种观点，可能会引用其他文献中的语段，导致文献内容混杂，逻辑难以辨析。

二、历史文献翻译的原则与技巧

由于大部分历史文献具有高度的专业性和权威性，译者必须保证译文的准确性和可读性。在历史文献中含有大量的文化负载词，承载着丰富的文化内涵，因而成为历史文献翻译的主要难点。译者应当做好一切译前准备，理解语篇中的文化负载词所蕴含的背景信息，从而保证译文的准确性。此外，历史文献中存在大量的长难句和复合句，需要译者仔细剖析其成分，在背景知识的辅助下，正确理解其含义。在一些历史文献中，可能存在大量代词的情况，译者可通读全文，在明晰全文大意的基础上，选择符合目的语语言表达习惯的方式进行翻译。

第二节　专业术语与常用表达

1.雅利安人	Aryans
2.种族融合	Admixture
3.盎格鲁-撒克逊人	Anglo-Saxon
4.阿拉伯人	Arab

续表

5.澳大利亚原住民	Australoid
6.孟加拉人	Bengalee
7.棕色人种	Brown peoples
8.布希曼人	Bushmen
9.迦南人	Canaanite
10.高加索人	Caucasian
11.彻罗基人	Cherokees
12.荷兰人	Dutch
13.荷兰东印度公司	Dutch East India Company
14.爱斯基摩人	Esquimaux
15.斐济人	Fijians
16.赫梯人	Hittite
17.霍屯督人	Hottentots
18.哈德逊湾公司	Hudson's Bay Company
19.《人类种族》	Human Species
20.易洛魁族	Iroquois
21.爪哇人	Javanese
22.卡菲尔部落	Kaffir tribes
23.大宪章	Magna Charta
24.马来人	Malay
25.毛利人	Maori
26.淡黑白色人种	Melanochroic
27.蒙古人	Mongoloid
28.黑白混血儿	Mulattoes
29.奥奈达人	Oneidas

续表

30. 巴布亚人	Papuan
31. 波斯人	Persian
32. 波利尼西亚人	Polynesian
33. 葡萄牙人	Portuguese
34. 红印第安人	Red Man
35. 皇家殖民地研究院	Royal Colonial Institute
36. 斯堪的纳维亚人	Scandinavians
37. 阿姆斯特丹	Amsterdam
38. 阿尔泰山脉	Altai mountains
39. 贝专纳兰	Bechuanaland
40. 海岸角城堡	Cape Coast Castle
41. 开普殖民地	Cape Colony
42. 弗里敦	Free Town
43. 恒河	Ganges
44. 瓜德罗普岛	Guadeloupe
45. 海地	Hayti
46. 喜马拉雅山脉	Himalayas
47. 伊斯帕尼奥拉岛	Hispaniola
48. 爪哇岛	Java
49. 拉哥斯	Lagos
50. 拉普兰德	Lapland

第三节　英译汉翻译实务

一、原文

The power of variation has been given to man to a degree which certainly prevents any feeling of monotony from arising when we survey the world. Colors and shades, statures, shapes of skull, angles of face, relative development of organs, and other physical differences, have been abundantly distributed; while as to languages and dialects, mental capacities, sentiments, dispositions and tempers, moral ideas and religious hopes and fears, of these we can but say that, like Cleopatra's charms, Age cannot stale nor custom wither their infinite variety.

The efforts of ethnologists to attain a satisfactory grouping of races have given rise to much interesting research and argument, and some lines of demarcation not difficult to follow have been attained, provided we bear in mind that the lines are not sharp-cut all over the field, although definite enough when extremes are brought into contiguity. One leading ethnologist has not been able to reduce the fundamental division to less than eleven; another requires fifteen; another, sixteen.

二、学生译文初稿

正是种族间存在的差异才让我们观察世界时不会觉得单调乏味。不同种族都具有千差万别的的肤色、身材体格、头骨形状、脸部轮廓并且器官的发育程度和身体的其他方面也不尽相同。而对于不同种族使用的语言、方言，拥有的心智情感、性情脾气、道德观念、宗教信仰的差异，我们只能说这些差异如同“克利欧佩特拉（Cleopatra）幻变的魅力”——“岁月无法磨灭她的风情万种，习俗也不能腐蚀她的仪态万千”。

人种学家试图对所有种族做出令人满意的分类。这一尝试催生了大量有趣的实验研究和观点看法，并且对显而易见的种族间差异也已划定。但我们仍需明白种族间的界限划分绝非泾渭分明（尽管当截然不同的种族同时出现，种族差异一目了然）。因此，一位人种学界的领军学者可能至少将人类种族划分为11种，而其他人种学者可能又划分为15种或16种。

——译员：牛婷

三、学生译文修改稿

正是种族间存在的差异才让我们观察世界时不会觉得单调乏味。不同种族都具有千差万别的的肤色、身材体格、头骨形状、脸部轮廓、器官的发育程度以及身体的种种方面。而对于不同种族使用的语言、方言，拥有的心智情感、性情脾气、道德观念、宗教信仰的差异，我们只能说这些差异如同“埃及艳后（Cleopatra）幻变的魅力”——“岁月无法磨灭她的风情万种，习俗也不能腐蚀她的仪态万千”。

人种学家试图对所有种族进行完美的分类。这一尝试催生了大量有趣的实验研究以及相关争论，并且对显而易见的种族间差异也有所划定。尽管截然不同的种族有着一目了然的种族差异，但我们仍需明白，种族间的界限划分绝非泾渭分明。因此，一位人种研究界的领军者可能将人类种族划分为至少 11 种，而其他人种学者可能又将其划分为 15 种或 16 种。

审校人：张静&杨雯
审校时间：2020.4.16

删除[饭]: 并且

删除[饭]: 和

删除[饭]: 身体的其他方面也不尽相同

删除[饭]: 克利欧佩特拉

删除[饭]: 做出令人满意的分类

删除[饭]: 和观点看法

删除[饭]: 已

删除[饭]: （尽管当截然不同的种族同时出现，种族差异一目了然）

删除[饭]: 学

删除[饭]: 学

删除[饭]: 至少

四、学生译文终稿

正是种族间存在的差异才让我们观察世界时不会觉得单调乏味。不同种族都具有千差万别的肤色、身材体格、头骨形状、脸部轮廓、器官的发育程度以及身体的种种方面。而对于不同种族使用的语言、方言，拥有的心智情感、性情脾气、道德观念、宗教信仰的差异，我们只能说这些差异如同“埃及艳后（Cleopatra）幻变的魅力”——“岁月无法磨灭她的风情万种，习俗也不能腐蚀她的仪态万千”。

人种学家试图对所有种族进行完美的分类。这一尝试催生了大量有趣的实验研究以及相关争论，并且对显而易见的种族间差异也有所划定。尽管截然不同的种族有着一目了然的种族差异，但我们仍需明白，种族间的界限划分绝非泾渭分明。因此，一位人种研究界的领军者可能将人类种族划分为至少 11 种，而其他人种学者可能又将其划分为 15 种或 16 种。

审校人：张静&杨雯
审校时间：2020.4.16

五、参考译文

正是人种差异才让人们在观察世界时不会觉得单调乏味。不同人种肤色各异，且身材体格、头骨形状、面部轮廓以及器官发育等不尽相同。语言方言丰富多样、心智情感发展各异、性情脾气迥然不同、道德观念及宗教信仰也大相径庭，我们只能说这些差异如同克利欧佩特拉幻变的魅力——“岁月无法磨灭她的风情万种，习俗也不能腐蚀她的仪态万千”。

人种学家尝试根据人种差异进行人种划分，从而催生大量实验研究及相关争论。尽管种族之间存在明显差异，但这也绝非泾渭分明。有的学者划分为11种，又有学者划分为15种或16种。

第四节　汉译英翻译实务

一、原文

由于欧洲各国的殖民运动已经蔓延至整个世界，欧洲殖民扩张注定成为雅利安运动的尾声。欧洲染指殖民的土地包括雅利安人当下生活的地区以及仍将受雅利安人掌控的土著人种的居住地（这些土著因被殖民才为人所知）。尽管欧洲殖民的土地仍有扩张的可能，但其拓殖的大致走向已有预设。在有限的能力范围内，试图分析并总结雅利安拓殖运动对全世界不同种族意味着什么注定是徒劳无益的。但仍需考虑，该运动是如何影响非雅利安种族的。

二、学生译文初稿

Since European colonization has spread all over the world, the expansion is meant to be the ending of Aryan movement. Land colonized by European countries includes the district that Aryan live on as well as that of indigenous people, who are famous because of colonization. Although there exists a chance for European expansion, the main trend has been preset. Within our limited ability, it will be in a vain to analyze and conclude the meaning of Aryan movement to different nationalities around the world. But we have to consider how it made an influence on non-Aryan nationalities.

——译员：张胜霞

三、学生译文修改稿

Since there is no new place to seize, European colonization is meant to be the ending period of Aryan movement. It already occupied those regions where Aryan used to live as well as those of indigenous people, who are known by us because of the colonization. Although there exists a chance for European expansion, the main trend has been laid down. Within our limited ability, it will be in a vain to analyze and conclude the meaning of Aryan movement to different races around the world. But we have to consider how it made an influence on non-Aryan races.

审校人：张静&杨雯

审校时间：2020.4.16

删除[T]: has spread all over the world, the expansion

删除[T]: Land

删除[T]: colonized by European countries includes the district that

删除[T]: on

删除[T]: that

删除[T]: famous

删除[T]: preset

删除[T]: nationalities

删除[T]: nationalities

设置格式[T]: 右

四、学生译文终稿

Since there is no new place to seize, European colonization is meant to be the ending period of Aryan movement. It already occupied those regions where Aryan used to live as well as those of indigenous people, who are known by us because of the colonization. Although there exists a chance for European expansion, the main trend has been laid down. Within our limited ability, it will be in a vain to analyze and conclude the meaning of Aryan movement to different races around the world. But we have to consider how it made an influence on non-Aryan races.

审校人：张静&杨雯

审校时间：2020.4.16

五、参考译文

European colonization is the latest phase of the Aryan movement, as there is now no fresh field to occupy. At least, it already concerns all those regions where the Aryan can live and continue to possess the characters by which we know him, and it must therefore be the beginning of the last movement of Aryans; its volume maybe increased, but all the probable lines of direction seem to be already laid down. There would be no gain from an attempt to analyse and summarize within our brief limits what this movement has meant for all the races of the world, but our subject requires some consideration of the way in which it has affected such non-Aryan branches of the human family as have been brought.

第五节　翻译实务评析

一、词法分析

在历史文献中，尤其是英语文本中，常出现大量的专有名词或文化负载词。其中，专有名词包括人名、地名、重大历史事件名称等，需要译者将其整理为术语表，构建专门的语料库，以便保证全文的统一性；文化负载词是体现历史文献文化内涵的重要载体，译者在充分查证文化负载词内涵之后，根据“信达雅”的翻译原则进行翻译，以保证历史文献的文化性。例如，在英译汉翻译实务中，原文仅出现英文单词“differences”，表示差异，而联系上下文，原文选自《大英殖民帝国》，是一本兼具文化性与可读性的历史文本。因此，译者应按照目的语语言在历史文本中的表达习惯，选择较为文雅的四字格进行翻译，将此单词译为“千差万别”。当然，参考译文完成得更加出色，将其译为“不尽相同、丰富多样、发展各异、迥然不同、大相径庭”。

二、句法分析

汉语中常见无主句，但不影响读者的阅读。而在英语中，大部分句子都包含主语和谓语，例如：在汉译英翻译实务中，原文“在有限的能力范围内，试图分析并总结雅利安拓殖运动对全世界不同种族意味着什么注定是徒劳无益的”缺少主语，为方便读者理解，译文根据上下文语境，补充了第一人称对ability进行修饰，将其译为“Within our limited ability, it will be in a vain to analyze and conclude the meaning of Aryan movement to different nationalities around the world.”同时，为避免头重脚轻，设置it作为形式主语。

三、语篇分析

语篇层面最为重要的文本要素为衔接和连贯。译文通顺且逻辑分明才具备其可读性，因此译文离不开衔接词和转折词。在翻译中，译者需要根据实际语境，采取增词或省词法，使得上下文衔接连贯，力求准确传达原文作者的含义。

【课外拓展】

研学活动中，历史博物馆的解说员向来自国外的学生们介绍“马踏飞燕”，请你与团队模拟情境，进行翻译。

文献参考

[1]黄国文．典籍翻译：从语内翻译到语际翻译——以《论语》英译为例[J]．中国外语，2012，9(06)：64-71．

[2]黄忠廉．翻译项目管理[M]．北京：国防工业出版社，2014．

[3]蒋骁华．典籍英译中的“东方情调化翻译倾向”研究——以英美翻译家的汉籍英译为例[J]．中国翻译，2010，31(04)：40-45+95．

[4]罗选民，杨文地．文化自觉与典籍英译[J]．外语与外语教学，2012(05)：63-66．

[5]李锦，廖开洪．文化语境顺应与翻译策略[J]．语言与翻译，2005(2)：49-52．

[6]李元胜．顺应论在中国的研究综述[J]．成都大学学报(教育科学版)，2007(3)：123-126。

[7]李占喜．国内外语用翻译研究：回顾、述评与前瞻[J]．上海翻译，2008(1)：20-26．

[8]梅晓娟，周晓光．选择、顺应、翻译——从语言顺应论角度看利玛窦西学译著的选材和翻译策略[J]．中国翻译，2008(2)：26-29+96．

[9]魏晓红，李清源．典籍英译中的文化语境顺应研究[J]，外语教学，2010(2)：109-112．

[10]王雪明，杨子．典籍英译中深度翻译的类型与功能——以《中国翻译话语英译选集》(上)为例[J]．中国翻译，2012，33(03)：103-108．

[11]徐珺，霍跃红．典籍英译：文化翻译观下的异化策略与中国英语[J]．外语与外语教学，2008(07)：45-48．

[12]周红民，程敏．回译：语言回归亦是真——一篇历史文献回译中的汉语体验[J]．上海翻译，2016(05)：25-32．